The ma[...]
Union Ca[...]
shown here. A separate volume details
the canal from Birmingham to Gayton

Northampton

Milton Keynes

Leighton Buzzard

Aylesbury

Wendover

Hemel Hempstead

Watford

Slough

LONDON

Published by Waterways World Ltd,

151 Station Street, Burton-on-Trent, Staffordshire DE14 1BG, England.
Revised and Edited by Euan Corrie
Designed by Michelle Hunt
Original Research by Marcus Potts
Maps by Branch Out Design, Bretby, Burton-on-Trent
All rights reserved: No part of this book may be reproduced in any form without the permission of the publisher.
Maps based on Ordnance Survey material reproduced by permission of Ordnance Survey on behalf of
The Controller of Her Majesty's Stationery Office, © Crown Copyright 100040026.
Third Edition 2004

One of a series of guides covering the Inland Waterways of England and Wales

British Library Cataloguing in Publication Data
A Catalogue Record for this book is available from the British Library
ISBN 1 870002 51 2
Printed in England by Information Press, Oxford

This Guide covers in detail the Grand Union Canal from Gayton Junction, in Northamptonshire, to the Thames at Brentford, its branches, including the Northampton Arm to the river Nene, Paddington Branch to Little Venice, in London, and the Regent's Canal onwards to Limehouse Basin, formerly Regent's Canal Dock. Also detailed are the Aylesbury, Wendover and Slough arms.

This new edition has been thoroughly revised and everything that the boater and towpath walker needs to know about this historic canal should be found in its pages.

It contains information about navigating the waterway, facilities for boating and shopping, and places of interest within walking distance of the canal. Moreover, towpath walkers and those who enjoy exploring canals by car are also catered for. So, whatever your interests are, we hope that you will find this guide useful. Have a good trip, remember the Country Code and enjoy discovering the southern part of the Grand Union system.

Acknowledgements

The editor is grateful to a great many people who have assisted in the production of this guide. In particular John Glock for being in the right place; Marcus Potts and Julie Lloyd undertook much research, Philippa Corrie acted as boat captain, car navigator, clerk and secretary on subsequent trips. Thanks are also due to the staff of British Waterways and the Aylesbury Canal Society's Laundrette List is, as always, an invaluable aid.

The Grand Junction – A Brief History

Today we think of the Grand Union Canal as a single, continuous waterway under the administration of one navigation authority, British Waterways. But it has not always been so. The history of our canals is both complex and fascinating and the section of the Grand Union Canal covered by this guide is no exception.

As the canal era progressed three separate canals were built which today form the main part of the Grand Union Canal – the Warwick & Birmingham Canal, the Warwick & Napton (originally the Warwick & Braunston) and the Grand Junction Canal. So far as this guide is concerned it is the Grand Junction Canal in which we are mainly interested since this was the original name of the canal which linked Braunston with the Thames at Brentford.

Before the construction of the Grand Junction Canal between Braunston and Brentford the main waterway route between the Midlands and the South and London was via the Oxford Canal (completed in 1790) and the river Thames. Clearly, a more direct route was needed to transport the rapidly increasing commerce spawned by the Industrial Revolution. The old route was circuitous, narrow-locked on the Oxford Canal, and subject to the seasonal fluctuations of drought and flood on the Thames, which was not then the well maintained waterway it is today.

In 1792 a survey was made for a canal

from the Oxford Canal at Hampton Gay to the Thames at Isleworth. This would still have involved using much of the narrow-locked Oxford Canal and it was rejected in favour of the present route from the Oxford Canal at Braunston to the Thames at Brentford. The route chosen offered many physical obstacles to canal construction. Inspection of a map reveals that the

The powered swing bridge at Winkwell beside the *Three Horseshoes* pub is one of the few remaining swing bridges on the Grand Union.

canal's route southwards from Braunston descends into the valleys of the rivers Nene and Great Ouse before climbing over the Chilterns and finally falling to the Thames. The canal would not have a single summit level, as is the case with many others built across a single hill range, but two. All this would require the construction of many locks, tunnels and aqueducts.

From the start in 1793 to its completion in 1805 the Grand Junction offered almost insuperable difficulties to its engineer William Jessop and his assistant James Barnes, particularly in tunnelling through the difficult ironstone outcrops at Braunston and Blisworth. Blisworth Tunnel held up completion for several years and a tramway was built over the hill to connect the two parts of the canal which had been completed. The Chilterns also presented problems but, instead of a tunnel, the long and deep cutting at Tring was constructed.

There were also problems with aqueducts. In 1806 the embankment leading to the original stone aqueduct over the Great Ouse at Wolverton burst and flooded the surrounding valley. The breach was repaired but, in 1808, the aqueduct itself collapsed and was

replaced, first, by a temporary wooden trunk, and then, in 1811, by the present iron trough. During the time that reconstruction was in progress the locks, which had earlier been built as a temporary means of carrying the canal across the Ouse, were brought back into use.

The construction of the Grand Junction Canal was, in its time, a work of the greatest magnitude, especially bearing in mind that there was no mechanical equipment (not even steam powered machines) to handle the thousands of tons of earth and rock which had to be moved. All this was moved by men and horses and there was loss of life, especially in the construction of the tunnels. In turn the Grand Junction Canal Company became the largest joint stock company in the world.

The Grand Junction was built as a wide-locked waterway which could be used by either barges or narrowboats, the latter often working in pairs. Here again it is worth emphasising that all were horse-drawn. Mechanical means of propulsion did not come until many years later. After its completion in 1805 the Grand Junction became very busy – it was the M1 of its time, affording a direct waterway link between the industrial Midlands and the Thames long before the first steam

Three pairs of loaded narrowboats lie against the towpath at Brentford in the 1950s, a few hundred yards above the Gauging Locks, ready to start their journeys up the Grand Union Canal. The wharves in the background have all now been swamped by modern luxury apartments.

train or long distance lorry followed the same route.

Numerous branches were built off the main line, linking the Grand Junction with such places as Northampton, Buckingham, Aylesbury, Wendover and Paddington. The last, to Slough, was completed in 1882. Braunston developed as an important canal centre with boat-building yards, warehouses and wharves while, all along the canal, new industries and activities rapidly developed because of the availability of cheap water transport.

The Regent's Canal

The Regent's Canal, completed in 1820, linked the Paddington Arm of the Grand Junction to the Thames at Limehouse. Often referred to as 'London's Canal' the Regent's (named after the Prince Regent) and the Regent's Canal Dock gave the Grand Junction a seaward terminus which, for many years, was very important, enabling canal craft to load direct overside from ships and take goods

through to the Midlands without transhipment. It traverses one side of Regent's Park and has three tunnels. For many years all its wide locks were in pairs.

The Grand Union – Amalgamation and Modernisation

With the development of the railways, many canals came under railway control. There was a great need to modernise the main routes of the canal system to compete with the new and faster mode of transport. One way of accomplishing this was for canal companies to amalgamate. The Grand Junction Co had acquired the Leicestershire & Northamptonshire Union Canal and the old Grand Union Canal (better known today simply as part of the 'Leicester Section') in 1894 and, in 1929, there was a greater amalgamation when the Regent's Canal, the Grand Junction, the Warwick & Napton and the Warwick & Birmingham amalgamated to form the unified Grand Union canal system – over 270 miles of canal under one control. The whole system, with others added in 1932, was known as the Grand Union Canal. From then on the name Grand Junction, which formed the longest single section of the new unified waterway disappeared into the history books.

Between 1930 and 1935 the new company set about modernising the canal and widening locks on the northern sections beyond Braunston so that there were wide locks all the way through from London to Birmingham.

All this was, of course, before the days of pleasure boating. The amalgamations and modernisations were undertaken to improve the canal for commerce and speed up the movement of working boats. Unlike some other canals, the Grand Union remained busy into the 20th century. A large fleet of carrying boats was built in the 1930s to coincide with the modernisation programme and during the Second World War the Grand Union was a vital artery which carried millions of tons of traffic.

After the war came nationalisation and the GU was transferred, along with most of the canal system, to the British Transport Commission's Docks & Inland Waterways Executive. Later this was split up and the canals were separately administered by British Transport Waterways. Not only were the canals nationalised but also the main carrying fleets, including that operated by the Grand Union Canal Carrying Co. Sadly traffic declined sharply and the number of working boats on the GU decreased. New carrying companies were established by people who believed in the future of water transport, but they were short-lived and, as old industries closed, the volume of trade on the canal fell further. Nevertheless, the Grand Union carried working boats longer than most other canals.

In 1962 the Grand Union, along with other canals, was transferred to the newly formed British Waterways Board. By this time commercial traffic was at a low ebb but pleasure boating had become a well established secondary use. By the end of the '60s there were more pleasure craft than working boats and under the terms of the 1968 Transport Act the Grand Union Canal was classified as a cruising waterway to be developed primarily for use by pleasure craft.

Working narrowboats could still be seen from time to time carrying coal southwards from collieries near Coventry to factories in the London area. The last regular long distance trade ceased in 1970. Thereafter, only an occasional working boat could be seen and today they are few and far between, trade having either disappeared with the closure of old industries or been transferred to the motorways and railways which follow a parallel route. Today the old Grand Junction section of the Grand Union Canal is a popular pleasure cruising waterway with numerous hire cruiser companies, marinas and cruising clubs established along its route. There are probably now more pleasure craft using it, especially in the summer months, than there were working boats in its heyday. More of the history of the Grand Junction and the Grand Union canals may be discovered at the Canal Museum situated beside the Grand Union Canal at Stoke Bruerne, details of which may be found in this guide.

History moves on and readers will find that we have tried to strike a balance between recording the history of the waterway as it remains visible on the ground and the many modern changes. Notable amongst these is the fact that British Waterways have applied bridge name plates and signs at locks which often diverge from those in use only 20 years ago, especially in the Apsley/Nash area and on the Aylesbury Arm. We have tried to find space for both tradition and progress on the maps and trust that the reader will find the result helpful.

Licences

Addresses of all the navigation authorities and other organisations which can provide further information are listed on page 15.

River Thames

No special licence is required to pass through the Pool of London (between the Regent's Canal at Limehouse, the river Lee at Bow Creek and the Grand Union at Brentford). But see also the guidance offered on pages 90–91 for passage of the tideway.

Craft hoping to proceed further upstream, through Teddington Lock and beyond, will require a licence for passage of the non-tidal Thames. Registration forms and details of charges may be obtained from the Environment Agency at Reading (See Useful Addresses on page 15). Transit Licences are also issued by the lock keepers at Teddington Lock (for boats joining the river from the tideway, at Osney (for craft joining the river from the Oxford Canal), and at Blakes Lock for those entering from the Kennet & Avon Navigation). The Environment Agency and British Waterways (see below) jointly offer a 'Gold Licence' for craft regularly using both authorities' waterways.

Grand Union Canal

All craft, whether powered or unpowered, including canoes and dinghies, must have a British Waterways Boat Licence when navigating the Grand Union Canal, or indeed, the rest of the connected canal system. Details of licensing are obtainable from the Waterway Managers at Norwood Top Lock or Marsworth Junction or from British Waterways' Watford headquarters. (See Useful Addresses on page 15.)

Some canal-based hire cruisers may carry a Thames as well as a British Waterways Licence, but hirers should check this in advance with the boatyard proprietor if they wish to navigate the river as well as the canal.

Navigation Notes

Stoppages

From time to time, particularly in the winter months (November–March), it may become necessary for British Waterways to carry out maintenance work on the waterway. Alternatively, a dry spring or summer may result in restrictions due to shortage of water. Either of these circumstances may result in sections being closed or 'stopped'. Details of Stoppages are published monthly in *Waterways World* magazine. For unscheduled stoppages telephone Canalphone South (01923 201402). To obtain assistance or report emergencies outside office hours dial 0800 4799947 for Freephone Canals. Have details of the waterway and the nearest lock or bridge number or similar landmark ready.

Water

The Braunston and Tring summits of the Grand Union Canal and the locks approaching them have been plagued throughout their history by shortage of water, and this is still a problem. No matter what the prevailing weather conditions the canal will always be short of water – CONSERVE IT! Share locks, wait for oncoming boats if the lock is in their favour (even if it costs you five minutes, that's better than a dry pound!) and always ensure that all the gates and paddles are closed before leaving a lock unless an approaching boat obviously intends to use it.

Speed

There is a speed limit of 4mph on the canal. Even this low speed is often too fast. Remember – an excessive wash or breaking wave causes bank erosion and damage to moored craft as well as being a general nuisance. If the wash from the stern starts to break up the banks EASE OFF, and you'll probably find that your speed in relation to terra-firma will increase anyway. Slow down when approaching or passing moored craft, other craft under way, locks, bridges, tunnels, engineering works and on bends. When the view ahead is obstructed, slow down, sound your horn and listen.

Rules of the Road

Craft meeting should steer to the right and pass each other left to left. If you do not intend to do this you must make it clear to the oncoming boat. When a vessel is being towed from the bank pass outside the vessel to avoid fouling the towing line – never pass between the towed vessel and the bank. Craft travelling with the current on rivers or tideway have the right of way over those heading against the flow.

Since the GU is considered a barge canal throughout much of the length covered by this guide, steerers of narrowboats should prepare themselves for the occasional encounter with broad-beamed craft. Show due consideration and allow them the benefit of deeper water where it exists, especially on bends and when approaching bridges. Also bear in mind that they are likely to be less manoeuvrable than you. Though now a rare sight, loaded working boats, both broad and narrow beam, should be awarded similar respect.

Depth

If you could see the canal drained of its water you'd be surprised how shallow it is, especially at the edges, the cross section being a shallow 'V' rather than 'U' shaped. Keep to the centre of the channel except when passing oncoming boats. Give way to larger craft, which require deeper water. You may find yourself aground if you have moved out of the centre channel to meet another boat. This is nothing to worry about. You should be able to reverse off, but if that doesn't work, push yourself off with your boat pole.

Flooding

Having pointed out the problems of water shortages, it may sound contradictory to raise the topic of flooding. This too can be a hazard after heavy rain. Between Stoke Bruerne and Cosgrove the canal is fed by the river Tove; below Boxmoor the Gade enters and it and the Chess add to the canal's waters from there to Uxbridge; finally, The Brent enters below Hanwell Locks. If there has been a lot of rain these river sections rise dramatically and in places flow quite fiercely. When this happens extra care will be needed, especially heading downstream through bridges.

Mooring

On rivers always moor with your bows pointing up-stream and allow sufficient slack on mooring lines to compensate for changes in level. The current is always faster through bridge arches and between bridge piers so do not attempt to turn up-stream of bridges.

Always, unless specifically indicated to the contrary, moor against the towpath side of the canal. Steer your boat in bow first, put the engine into neutral and then pull the stern of your boat in with your rope. Keeping the propeller turning near to the bank could seriously damage the propeller and both the bed and bank of the canal. When pushing off again, ensure that the boat is well away from the bank before engaging forward gear.

East of Acton Lane on the Regent's and Paddington section the towpath has been adopted as an electricity cableway, the high-voltage lines lying hidden beneath pre-cast concrete slabs. The slabs provide an excellent walking surface but do not make for easy mooring.

- *Do not* moor too near bridges or locks so as to obstruct full size craft cruising the canal.

- *Do not* moor on bends or in winding holes.

- *Do not* moor in the short pounds of a flight of locks.

- *Do not* stretch ropes across towpaths where they will obstruct and endanger towpath users.

Navigation

Safety First

Remember always that prevention is better than cure. Wear non-slip footwear and beware of slippery lock sides and gates in wet weather. Beware of low bridges – some of which are lower in the middle (sometimes with supporting girders) than at each end. Make sure that your crew – especially those sitting on the cabin top – is aware of the presence of a low bridge. Before you enter a long tunnel, tell the crew to switch on the cabin lights (the cabin lights shining on the walls are useful to the helmsman). Ensure that torches are handy when entering tunnels and for use at night.

It is advisable to be able to swim when contemplating a holiday afloat. Non-swimmers and young children should wear life jackets. When walking along the side-decks hold the handrails on the cabin top.

Make sure that you know the position and method of operation of the fire extinguishers provided on the boat. Take a basic first aid kit with you including insect repellent. It is a good rule to spend the first night aboard making sure that you know where everything is, how emergency equipment works and reading the instructions or handbooks on essential equipment provided by the owner.

Tunnels

Canal craft should be equipped with a suitable headlamp for navigating tunnels. This should be trained slightly to the right to avoid dazzling oncoming steerers in wide tunnels. Torches should also be carried. Go dead slow when approaching other craft but do not stop in tunnels except in an emergency.

There are tunnels on the Regent's Canal at Islington, Lisson Grove and Maida Hill. These must be used on a one way system. If you see a boat approaching in the tunnel wait for it to clear as it may be a wide beam vessel which you cannot pass. On the (former Grand Junction Canal) main line there are tunnels at Blisworth (3,056 yards long, one of the country's longest), Braunston (2,042 yards) and Shrewley. You can expect to meet, and successfully pass, other narrow beam boats in these three tunnels. Unpowered craft are prohibited from passing through all of the tunnels.

Vessels exceeding 7ft beam should notify the relevant Waterway Managers if they intend to proceed through Braunston or Blisworth tunnels and must await authorisation (and stopping of opposing traffic) before attempting passage.

Bridges

Height

Several bridges have little headroom between cabin roof and brickwork. Boaters, particularly those with roof-top passengers, chimneys and tall pipes, are advised to look well ahead and play it safe rather than sorry!

Lift and Swing Bridges

Lift bridges are common on some canals such as the Llangollen or Oxford while others specialise in the swinging variety. Although visually often attractive, these, like low brick arches have their own special hazards for navigators. If you line your boat up with the coping on the towpath side of the bridge, the roof of your boat should miss the bridge decking, but if the wind catches the boat, or the boat hits the coping and bounces off, you could hit your cabin. When approaching these bridges, never allow anyone to stand at the bows of the boat near to where the cabin might hit the bridge – several tons of boat travelling at up to 4mph could easily crush them between boat and bridge. Never attempt to get off the boat onto the deck of a moveable bridge, this has proved fatal several times. Use common sense when lifting or swinging the bridges and do not open the bridge if a vehicle is approaching. Where no gate is provided, a member of your crew should warn road traffic.

Only the Northampton Arm of the Grand

Union still retains its lift bridges and even these are usually fastened up, clear of passing boats.

Note: Do not stand on the roof of the boat or anywhere along the gunwale nearest the bridge deck when passing under lift bridges and never attempt to get off the boat onto the bridge deck.

BW Sanitary Station keys (Yale type)

It is essential to have at least one of these on board to gain access to Sanitary Stations and water points. Keys are available for purchase direct from British Waterways (see Useful Addresses, page 15) and from most boat yards and marinas.

Mileage

Gayton Junction to Bull's Bridge	71
Gayton Junction to Northampton	4¾
Bull's Bridge to Little Venice	13
Bull's Bridge to Brentford	6
Little Venice to Limehouse	8½
Aylesbury Arm, Marsworth to Aylesbury	6¼
Wendover Arm, Bulbourne to Tringford *(being increased by restoration)*	1¼
Slough Arm, Cowley to Slough	5

Locks

Lock Dimensions In canal parlance, the Grand Union main line and Regent's Canal are wide canals, meaning that the waterway, and more particularly the locks, were built to take two of the traditional English narrowboats side by side. The Northampton and Aylesbury arms have narrow locks capable of accommodating only one full length narrowboat at a time. Originally, broad boats traded regularly up the main line as far north as Braunston but nowadays their skippers must take great care when following their example particularly as described under 'Tunnels' on page 8.

Today, the lock dimensions are:

Grand Union Main Line: Camp Hill Top Lock, Birmingham to Brentford

Length	up to 72ft (21.9m)
Beam	up to 12ft 6in (3.8m)
Headroom	7ft 6in (2.2m)
Draught	up to 3ft (0.91m)

But, note that the Grand Union Canal Company's modernization scheme was never completed and while it is possible to get a 14ft beam boat through the locks between Brentford and Birmingham difficulty will be experienced with the offside of arched bridges. North of Braunston many of the bridges were never widened and at points such as Long Itchington 12ft 6in will be found to be a practical maximum beam. Local advice and information from British Waterways will be essential.

Northampton Arm: Gayton Junction to the Nene at Northampton

Length	up to 72ft (21.9m)
Beam	up to 7ft 0in (2.1m)
Draught	up to 3ft (0.91m)

Aylesbury Arm: Marsworth Junction to Aylesbury

Length	up to 72ft (21.9m)
Beam	up to 7ft 0in (2.1m)
Draught	up to 3ft (0.91m)

Paddington Arm: Bull's Bridge to Little Venice

Length	up to 72ft (21.9m)
Beam	up to 12ft 6in (3.8m)
Headroom	7ft 6in (2.2m)
Draught	up to 3ft (0.91m)

Regent's Canal: Little Venice to Limehouse

Length	up to 78ft (23.7m)
Beam	up to 14ft 6in (4.4m)
Headroom	8ft 6in (2.6m)
Draught	up to 4ft (1.2m)

Limehouse Ship Lock (for access to the marina in the former Regent's Canal Dock only)

Length	up to 98ft (29.8m)
Beam	up to 25ft 4in (7.7m)
Headroom	unlimited
Draught	up to 9ft (2.7m)

Brentford Gauging Locks to the Thames

Length   up to 95ft (28.9m)
Beam   up to 18ft 6in (5.6m)
Draught   up to 3ft 6in (1.1m)

Number of Locks

Gayton Junction to
    Brentford: 89
Gayton Junction to
    Northampton: 17
Marsworth to Aylesbury: 16
Marsworth to Wendover: 0
Cowley Peachey to Slough: 0
Bull's Bridge to Limehouse: 13

Lock Operation

The golden rule is never waste water. The lock drill described below should be followed systematically.

The basic principle of lock operation is that water never passes straight through a lock. It comes in from the top and stays in, or goes out through the bottom without any following it from the top. If you liken the lock itself to a kitchen sink – the top end to the tap and the bottom to the plug – don't turn the tap on until the plug is in, and don't pull the plug out until the tap is off.

Lock Keepers On the river Thames lock keepers are usually on hand to direct traffic and operate the lock. The British Waterways controlled locks at Thames Locks, Brentford, Limehouse Basin Entrance and Bow Tidal Locks are only operated by their keepers. British Waterways (see page 110) publish an essential leaflet detailing the hours when these locks are available. This is the exception; lock operation on canals is usually undertaken by the boat crew. At busy spots lock keepers may be available to assist and regulate traffic. They may ask you to share a lock with another boat or wait while another boat comes through the other way. Obey their instructions but

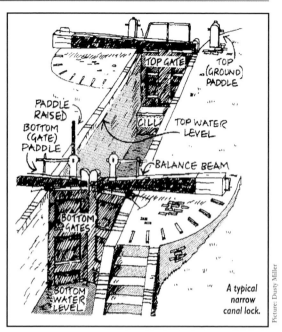

A typical narrow canal lock.

Picture: Dusty Miller

do not necessarily expect that they will do the work for you – that's part of the fun of your holiday.

Staircase Locks The only staircase locks on the part of the Grand Union Canal that is covered in this guide book are the pair at the head of the Aylesbury Arm at Marsworth.

A staircase lock is one where the top gate forms the bottom gate of the next chamber. These abound on the Leeds & Liverpool where they are often referred to as 'risers' and may be spotted at Foxton, Watford and Bascote on the Grand Union. Staircase locks are basically the same as ordinary locks and there is only one rule: When you're going up always make sure that the chamber above you is full (so that its water can be used to fill your chamber) and when you're going down check that the chamber below you is empty (so that the water from your chamber can be let into it). Only open the paddles between one chamber and one of its immediate neighbours at a time so as not to drain all the water from under your boat and do not try to empty a higher chamber into one below which is already full!

Several staircases have full time keepers to assist (but not that at Marsworth) so look for notices advising of their presence and take instructions before doing anything. Do not start working through staircase locks if a boat is already coming from the opposite direction.

How to Operate Locks

A windlass is usually required to fit the paddle spindles of manually operated locks. These will usually be provided on the boat and have two holes of different sizes to take the spindle's squared end. Take care to use the correct sized hole on the spindle as a bad fit is dangerous since the windlass may fly off. In direct contravention of the recommendation of its own paddle gearing committee British Waterways has fitted a mixture of sizes of spindles at numerous locks so constant attention is needed. Do not leave the windlass on the spindle when not winding the paddle up or down – make sure the pawl is in place to stop the paddle falling and remove the windlass so that it cannot fly round if the catch slips.

Those of the crew who operate the paddles must remember that the noise of the engine and rushing water will prevent people on the boat hearing their instructions, or them hearing shouts of panic. Those ashore are responsible for keeping an eye on the boat all the time that the lock is filling or emptying to see that it continues to rise or fall steadily. If there is any doubt, shut all the paddles quickly and then stop to think and check if the boat or its ropes and fenders are catching on any part of the lock or other boats. Particularly check that the stem fender does not catch under the top gate or its handrails when going up hill. Boats sharing locks, which is a good way to save water, must lie beside or ahead and astern of one another, *never* twisted across each other at bow or stern. Like

that they will jam as the level alters.

(1) Going Uphill – Lock Empty

Check that top paddles are closed.

Enter the lock and drive the boat to the far end where there will be less turbulence as the lock fills.

Close the bottom gates. See that the bottom gate paddles are closed.

Open top ground paddles (where applicable). Water from these will pass under the boat to the other end of the chamber and hold the boat steadily against the top gate or cill.

Ropes are not usually required to hold a boat steady in narrow locks but will often be a good idea in bigger chambers. A line used as a spring running slightly astern from the fore end may be best with some tension being maintained by keeping the engine running in forward gear. Do not tie knots in any rope used in locks, they will jam when it is necessary to adjust the length of line as the water rises or falls and leave the boat hanging in mid air or sunk. Do not try to hold a rope as the lock fills either; take a couple of turns round a cleat or bollard and the extra friction thus gained will help prevent the boat dragging the rope through your hand causing nasty burns as it does so.

In most wide beam locks, such as those on the Grand Union canal, where two or more narrowboats will fit alongside one another, a less turbulent ascent for a single boat, will result from drawing the top ground paddle on the same side as the boat first. The water will usually pass beneath the boat and help to hold it steadily against the wall.

Open the top gate paddles when their outlets in the gates are submerged (where applicable). Some locks have only gate paddles and greater care is needed here to avoid flooding the fore end of the boat by opening these too much too rapidly when going up hill .

When the lock is full open the top gates. Leave the lock. Close the top gates and all paddles.

Illustration: Dusty Miller

(2) Going Uphill – Lock Full

Check that there is no boat approaching from above the lock which could save water by descending as you empty the lock for your boat to enter.

If not, close the top gates. See that the top gate and ground paddles are closed. Open the bottom paddles.

When the lock is empty open the bottom gates and close the bottom gate paddles. Proceed as (1) above.

(3) Going Downhill – Lock Full

Enter the lock and drive the boat to the far end where it will be well clear of the cill near the top gates as the water drops.

Close the top gates. See that the top gate paddles and ground paddles are closed.

Open the bottom gate paddles.

When lock is empty open the bottom gates.

Leave the lock. Close all bottom paddles and gates.

(4) Going Downhill – Lock Empty

Check that there is no boat approaching from below the lock which could save water by ascending as you fill the lock for your boat to enter.

Close the bottom gates. See that the bottom gate paddles are closed.

Open the ground paddles.

Open the top gate paddles when submerged (where applicable).

When the lock is full, open the top gates. Proceed as (3) above.

Before leaving a lock see that all paddles are fully and securely closed. On canals it is important to shut the exit gates as well; failure to do so may result in serious flooding of property, stranding of craft through loss of water from the pound above, and possible flooding of craft when the pound is refilled.

Much discussion concerns the shutting of lock gates on the Grand Union, a debate which will almost certainly involve the user of this guide. In essence, leaving gates open can lead to low or even dry pounds. It is true that working boatmen left lock gates open, but there are several reasons why this practice should not be universal today: Primarily, traffic in the 2000s, though sometimes heavy, is no longer regular and intervals between boats at locks can sometimes be considerable. Similarly, night-time boating, is no longer approved, so a lock could be left with gates open for 10 hours or more. South of Hemel Hempstead, particularly through Apsley, by-weirs are generally inadequate and excess water tends to flow over lock gates. This means that a lock with gates shut will soon be out of level to any approaching boat, so demanding resetting either way. Such excessive water levels can flood towpaths and make opening gates, themselves over weir, very difficult. Officially, it is British Waterway's preference that both top and bottom gates (and paddles) should be closed when a boat leaves a lock unless another boat is approaching.

It is easiest to pick up lock crew at the lock mouth, which saves approaching the shallow canal margins where you may run aground. But in all situations where crew are joining or leaving even a slowly moving boat make them get on or off at the stern. Should they slip they will then get wet after the boat has passed and not fall in where it will pass over them or crush them against a wall. At the stern the steerer is also at hand to put the engine out of gear quickly and assist.

Beyond The Towpath

This publication is intended primarily as a guide to the canal but it also includes information on some of the places of interest near the canal. More detailed information can be obtained from local tourist offices. (See the text accompanying the maps and page 15 for details of Tourist Offices).

Walking The Grand Union Canal

Although canal towpaths are not usually Public Rights of Way, the public is now encouraged to make use of these excellent long-distance footpaths. Some very good canalside walks may be enjoyed by combining lengths of towpaths with the official footpaths and bridleways marked on the appropriate OS Landranger 1:50,000 maps covering the area. Many of these tracks and byways are also marked on the maps in this guide. Work has been done to improve the towpath along the Grand Union Canal. That along the main line now

forms part of a waymarked long-distance route. Where fences or gates cross the path walkers should leave them as they find them. Stout footwear is essential.

In general the Grand Union towpath is in good condition and the most frequent obstacle to be encountered is mud, especially in the deeper cuttings such as Tring or Dawley. As one nears London the situation improves further, largely due to the work instigated by the Canalway Project. The scheme was initiated by the GLC in 1978 and seen as a way of improving public access and appreciation of the canal through London. In recent years this has been extended further to encompass reclamation, rehabilitation and landscaping of the canal's immediate environs, largely to good effect. The result is an excellent towpath surface throughout the Greater London area and a noticeable improvement in accessibility. This is especially apparent through those areas controlled by Hillingdon and Westminster, though walkers are warned that access points to/from the Regent's Canal towpath may be locked between dusk and dawn. Boaters will discover that the standard BW service key should unlock these gates and are asked to re-close any such access points after use. Remember: the land on the opposite side of the canal to the towpath is almost certainly private property. Stay on the towpath or recognised footpaths and do not trespass.

General

Always respect the pleasure of other waterway users and the life of the countryside generally. Do not litter or pollute the waterways and always observe the Country Code –

- Guard against fire risks.
- Fasten all gates.
- Keep dogs under proper control.
- Keep to the paths across farm land.
- Avoid damaging fences, hedges and walls.
- Protect wildlife, wild plants and trees.
- Go carefully on country roads.

Bibliography

The Canals of the East Midlands by Charles Hadfield. David & Charles.

The Grand Junction Canal by Alan Faulkner. W.H. Walker & Bros 1993.

The Regent's Canal: London's Hidden Waterway by Alan Faulkner. Waterways World Ltd. To be published 2004.

Braunston to Brentford by Geoff Elwin & Cathleen King. Blackthorn Publications 1980.

The Grand Union Canal from the Chilterns to the Thames by Geoff Elwin & Cathleen King. Blackthorn Publications 1981.

London's Waterways by Martyn Denney. Batsford 1977.

Historic Waterway Scenes – London and South East England by Martyn Denney. Moorland 1980.

Bread upon the Waters by David Blagrove. J.M. Pearson & Son 1984.

Hold on A Minute by Tim Wilkinson. George Allen & Unwin 1965.

London's Waterway Guide by Chris Cove Smith. Imray 1977.

Through London by Canal. British Waterways 1977.

The Aylesbury Arm by Geoff Giddings and Liz Cooper. Aylesbury Canal Society 1996.

Water From Wendover – The Story of the Wendover Arm Canal by Shelley Savage. Wendover Arm Trust 2002.

The Grand Union Canal; in Hertfordshire by Alan Faulkner. Hertfordshire Publications 1987.

The Canal: Tring–Rickmansworth In Camera. Quotes Ltd, Buckingham 1987.

Exploring the Regent's Canal by Michael Essex Lopresti. Brewin 1994.

The Grand Union Canal Walk by Clive Holmes. Cicerone Press 1996.

The Grand Union Canal Walk by Anthony Burton and Neil Curtis. Aurum Press & British Waterways 1993.

Waterways World magazine: many articles on various aspects of the Grand Union Canal have been published in the monthly magazine *Waterways World* – details of which may be found in the magazine's indexes. Indexes and backnumbers of *Waterways World* are available by post from Waterways World Ltd, 151 Station Street, Burton-on-Trent, Staffordshire DE14 1BG. (01283 742950).

Maps and Charts

GEOprojects map of the Grand Union Canal – fold-out boater's map.

Stanford's *Map of the River Thames (Lechdale to Richmond).*

Imray's *Map of the River Thames (Teddington to Southend).*

Nicholson/Ordnance Survey Guides to the Waterways Volumes 1 London, Grand Union, Oxford and Lee and 7 Thames, Wey and Kennet & Avon.

Ordnance Survey Landranger 1:50,000 maps 152, 165, 166, 176 and 177 cover the route of the canals.

London A–Z Street Atlas

Note: British Waterways publish a range of information leaflets – copies of these may be obtained (free) from BW's offices – see under Useful Addresses.

Guides to adjoining canals

This guide links up with others in the series at Gayton Junction – the *Waterways World Guide to the Grand Union (North)*. (New edition in preparation.)

Other guides in the Waterways World Canal Guide series

Coventry, Ashby & Oxford (North) Canals (including the Birmingham & Fazeley)

Grand Union (Leicester Section)

Oxford Canal

Kennet & Avon Canal

Trent & Mersey Canal (including the Caldon Canal)

Llangollen Canal (including the Montgomery Canal)

Shropshire Union Canal

Staffs & Worcs Canal.

For availabilty, contact: Waterways World Ltd, 151 Station Street, Burton-on-Trent, Staffordshire DE14 1BG (01283 742950).

Useful Addresses

The Environment Agency, Thames Region: Kings Meadow House, Kings Meadow Road, Reading RG1 8DQ (0118 953 5525, www.visitthames.co.uk). Recorded navigation information 0118 953 5620.

The Port of London Authority (Responsible for the river Thames from Teddington to the sea): Bakers Hall, 7 Harp Lane, London EC3R 6LB (020 7743 7900, www.portoflondon.co.uk).

British Waterways

General Manager Grand Union Canal (Cowley to Stowe Hill), including the Northampton, Aylesbury and Wendover Arms: British Waterways, Ground Floor, Witan Gate House, 500-600 Witan Gate, Milton Keynes MK9 1BW (01908 302500, Fax: 01908 302510).

General Manager Grand Union Canal (Cowley Lock to Brentford and Limehouse) including the Slough Arm, Hertford Union and Regent's canals and Rivers Lee & Stort: British Waterways London Region, 1 Sheldon Square, Paddington Central, London W2 6TT (020 7985 7200, Fax: 020 7985 7201, enquiries.london@britishwaterways.co.uk).

Headquarters and Craft Licensing: British Waterways Willow Grange, Church Road, Watford, Hertfordshire WD17 4QA (01923 226422, Fax: 01923 201400).

BW's web site is www.britishwaterways.co.uk.

Tourist Information

London, Britain Visitor Centre: 1 Lower Regent Street, Piccadilly Circus, London SW1Y 4XT (personal callers only).

London, Islington: 44 Duncan Street, Islington, London N1 8BW (020 7278 8787, Fax 020 7833 2193, email: VIC@islvic.demon.co.uk.

London, Tower Hamlets: 18 Lamb Street, London E1 6EA (020 7375 2549, Fax 020 7375 2539)

Aylesbury: 8 Bourbon Street, Aylesbury, Buckinghamshire HP20 2RR (01296 330559, email: info@aylesbury-tourist.org.uk).

Buckingham: The Old Gaol Museum, Market Hill, Buckingham MK18 1JX (01280 823020).

Hemel Hempstead: Marlowes, Hemel Hempstead, Hertfordshire HP1 1DT (01442 234222, Fax 01442 230427, www.dacorum.gov.uk).

Milton Keynes: Margaret Powell Square, 890 Midsummer Boulevard, Central Milton Keynes, Buckinghamshire MK9 3QA (01908 558300, Fax 01908 558316, www.imk.co.uk).

Northampton: Northampton Museum & Art Gallery, Guildhall Road, Northampton, NN1 1DP (01604 838800, www.northampton.go.uk).

Wendover: The Clock Tower, High Street, Wendover, Buckinghamshire HP22 6DU (01296 696759, Fax: 01296 622460).

Canal Societies

Inland Waterways Association, PO Box 114, Rickmansworth, Hertfordshire WD3 1ZY (01923 711114, Fax 01923 897000, email: iwa@waterways.org.uk, www. waterways.org.uk).

Aylesbury Canal Society, Canal Basin, Aylesbury, Buckinghamshire HP21 7QG (01923 779401, www.aylesburycanal.org.uk (Moorings in Aylesbury Basin).

Bedford & Milton Keynes Waterway Trust, c/o The Gables, Broughton, Milton Keynes, MK10 9AA (01908 663166, Fax 01908 691707, email: info@b-mkwaterway.org.uk, b-mkwaterway.org.uk.

Buckingham Canal Society, 18 Elmers Park, Old Bletchley, Milton Keynes MK3 6DJ (01908 674317, www.mkheritage.co.uk/bcs).

Leighton Buzzard Canal Society, 41 Himley Green, Linslade, Bedfordshire LU7 2PY (01525 374498).

Contacts

Wendover Arm Trust, 80 Ashfield, Stantonbury, Milton Keynes MK14 6AT (01908 311521).

Hire Boat Companies operating on the southern part of the Grand Union Canal

Association of Pleasure Craft Operators, Parkland House, Audley Avenue, Newport, Shropshire TF10 7BX. (01952 813572, Fax 01952 820363, email apco@bmif.co.uk, www.bmif.co.uk), will provide information on boat hirers on the Grand Union and elsewhere.

Alvechurch Boat Centres, (0121 445 2909, www.alvechurch.com). Craft based at Gayton Marina.

Blisworth Tunnel Boats, Unit 2W, Mill Wharf, Gayton Road, Blisworth, Northamptonshire NN7 3BN (01604 858868, www.blisworthtunnelboats. co.uk).

Wyvern Shipping Co, Rothschild Road, Linslade, Leighton Buzzard, Bedfordshire LU7 2TF (01525 372355, www. canalholidays.co.uk).

Canalboat Holidays, The Boatyard, Weedon, Northamptonshire NN7 4QD (01327 340739, email: info@canalboat-holidays.com, www. canalboat-holidays.co.uk).

Nationwide Narrowboats, 86 Wingfield Road, Tebworth, Bedfordshire LU7 9QQ (01525 874335, www.canaljunction.com/ nationwide) craft from Willowbridge Marina, Bletchley.

Union Canal Carriers, The Pump House, Canal Side, Little Braunston, Northamptonshire NN11 7HJ (01788 890784, www.unioncanlcarriers.co.uk). Based on the Grand Union Canal.

Weltonfield Narrowboats, Welton Hythe, Daventry, Northamptonshire NN11 5LG (01327 842282, email: enquiries@weltonfield.co.uk, www. weltonfield.co.uk).

Hotel Boats

Among the hotel boat operators that include the southern part of the Grand Union Canal in their itineraries are:

Inland Waterway Holiday Cruises, Greenham Lock Cottage, London Road, Newbury, Berkshire RG14 5SN (07831 110811).

Thames & Chiltern Holiday Cruisers, Rothbury House, High Street, Staithes, North Yorkshire TS13 5BQ (07966 248079).

Public Transport

Buses

The most comprehensive answers may be had by navigating the menu on National Express (Nationwide Services) www. nationalexpress.com, 08705 808080.

The National Traveline (0870 608 2 608) will provide rail or coach information nationally and local bus information.

Trains

Most stations near the Grand Union Canal between Wolverton and Watford lie on the Rugby–Euston main line. These include: Wolverton, Milton Keynes Central, Bletchley, Leighton Buzzard, Cheddington, Tring, Berkhamsted, Hemel Hempstead, Apsley, Kings Langley and Watford Junction.

Services on this line are frequent, especially during the morning and afternoon rush-hour periods.

At Bletchley branch-line trains link with Bedford and the Midland Main Line via Fenny Stratford. From Bedford connections with Leicester, Nottingham and the North East can be made.

At Watford branch-line trains link with St. Albans via Watford North. During rush hours services extend to Croxley Green.

From Watford to London Euston trains pass north east of the canal, not drawing near again until Stonebridge Park close to Park Royal. They then call at Harlesden,

Willesden Junction and Kensal Green along the Paddington Arm before swinging north to Primrose Hill and thence Euston. At Willesden the Rugby–Euston route crosses the Richmond–Broad Street line. Other than Gunnersbury Park it is of little use to the boater until it passes through Camden Road, Caledonian Road and Barnsbury, Highbury & Islington, Canonbury and Dalston Junction Stations. Of these, the last three lie 1 mile north of the Regent's Canal.

Several other lines are of interest. The Banbury–Marylebone route serves Denham but only links with Paddington during rush-hours. At such times trains also call at Ruislip, Northolt and Sudbury Hill. The Aylesbury–Marylebone line calls at Rickmansworth.

The Paddington–West Country route passes through Slough, Langley, Iver, West Drayton & Yiewsley, Hayes & Harlington, Southall and Hanwell before arriving in the City. Services to the smaller stations are only frequent during rush hours.

Routes from Liverpool Street serve the East End stations, including Cambridge Heath and Bethnal Green. Kings Cross and St. Pancras are of interest only in their own right, since no other stations on their lines are near the canal.

Service and fare details are best obtained from the National Enquiry service (08457 484950 or www.natinalrail.co.uk) which should also be able to give details of London Underground or Docklands Light Railway services.

Underground

From Watford to Brentford and Limehouse the Grand Union passes through an area exceptionally well served by public transport. In addition to buses and British Rail, London also benefits from the largest electrified underground system in the world. The complex underground network operates between 05:30 and 00:15 (23:30 on Sun), though some stations may close at weekends. Maps of the underground system are displayed at all tube stations and may be included in your diary.

London Transport

Transport For London is an umbrella body which provides excellent co-ordinated information about all types of transport and tickets within the Greater London Area. This extends to taxis and regular, timetabled, as well as charter river trips and ferries, the Docklands Light Railway and Croydon Tramlink. Telephone enquiries (24 hours): 020 722 1234, Information for disabled users: 020 7918 3015, and also at www.transportfor-london.gov.uk. In addition The Docklands Light Railway has a specific site at www.dlr.co.uk.

The Grand Union Canal – From Northampton to The Thames

It is hoped that inclusion of the Grand Union Canal's Arm to Northampton, which gives access to, or from, the river Nene, will improve the usefulness of this volume. Those approaching from further north are recommended to the Waterways World Cruising Guide to the Grand Union Canal (North). *The Nene is well covered by Imray's guide to the river.*

THE NORTHAMPTON ARM

Historical Introduction

The general history of the Grand Union Canal is described on pages 2–5.

A branch from the mainline to serve Northampton was included in the original Grand Junction Canal Act of 1793. The cost of construction and the potential demand for lockage water to be taken from the main line discouraged the company from building this link for 22 years. Further discouragement was caused by the failure of the Leicestershire & Northamptonshire Union Canal to complete its waterway from Market Harborough to Northampton as intended. Different lines for the branch were surveyed by Jessop and Barnes and estimates obtained from Benjamin Outram for a railroad from Blisworth. Eventually pressure from Northampton interests and the river Nene Commissioners coupled with the availability of second hand tramway rails from Blisworth and Wolverton secured a start. The railroad was opened on 7th October 1805. Northampton Corporation continued to campaign for a canal branch and by opposing other Grand Junction schemes eventually forced the canal company to give way. The narrow-locked branch was opened amid much ceremony on 1st May 1815 and was an immediate success. What became of the railway is not known although materials from it were still being offered for sale in 1824.

Gayton ☏ ⛽ 🍴 🛁

It's rather a climb to the village but there are two pubs to offer refreshment: the *Queen Victoria Inn* is a free house with a garden and skittles, serving Charles Wells and Badger ales and offering food every lunchtime and evening as well as all day Fri–Sun. The *Eykyn Arms* is a cheerful local pub serving Charles Wells beers but it does not open at Monday lunchtimes. Gayton Stores is open 9am–5pm. Early Closing Wed. Sat/Sun 10am–12 noon.

Gayton Junction

🛁 ⛽ 🛢 🍴 ♿ 〜

There's a BW yard here with services and slipway. Though now accompanied by a new bypass, the arm is one of he most beautiful stretches of canal anywhere in the country, and the narrowness of the canal and its seventeen locks come as a refreshing change from the main line.

On the offside approaching Milton Road Bridge (2) is Canal House once home and office of T.W Milner, the Grand Junction Canal Company's Northern District Engineer from 1895 until 1929 who left a vast resource of letters, reports and photographs for future historians of this waterway.

Grand Junction Boat Co ⛽ 🛢 📻

are all adjacent, boatbuilding and fitting out including gas fitting, repairs, breakdowns and Boat Safety Scheme inspections are catered for, occupies part of the former maintenance yard at Gayton Wharf, Northamptonshire, 01604 858043, Nene licences and security keys are available.

Alvechurch Boat Centres ⛽ 🍴 🛢 🌀

♿ ⛽ 🗑 📻 🛢 (01604 858685, www.alvechurch.com). Long term and temporary moorings and hire craft, hard standing, cranage, souvenir shop, temporary moorings, boatbuilding, fitting, repairs and brokerage, river Nene licences and keys.

MAP 1
Gayton Junction

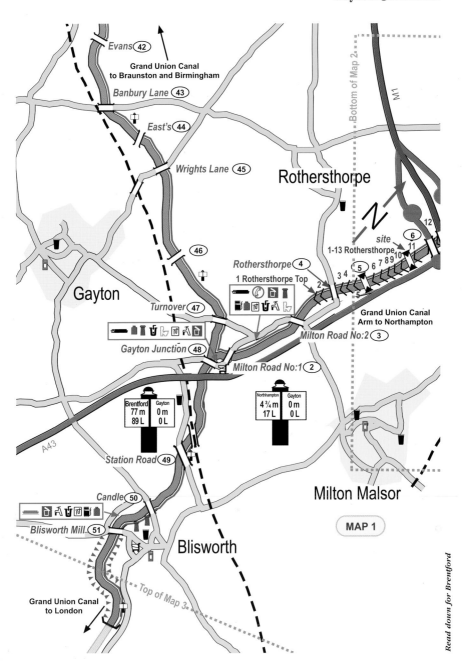

Evans (42)

Grand Union Canal
to Braunston and Birmingham

Banbury Lane (43)

East's (44)

Wrights Lane (45)

Rothersthorpe

(46)

Rothersthorpe (4)

1 Rothersthorpe Top

Turnover (47)

Gayton Junction (48)

Gayton

Milton Road No:2 (3)

Milton Road No:1 (2)

site
1-13 Rothersthorpe

Grand Union Canal
Arm to Northampton

Brentford	Gayton
77 m	0 m
89 L	0 L

Northampton	Gayton
4¾ m	0 m
17 L	0 L

Station Road (49)

Candle (50)

Blisworth Mill (51)

Blisworth

Milton Malsor

MAP 1

Grand Union Canal
to London

Top of Map 3

A43

Bottom of Map 2

M1

Read down for Brentford

Robin Smithett

Only one lift bridge now remains among Rothersthorpe Locks on the Northampton Arm and it is rare for boat crews to find that closed against them.

Rothersthorpe 🄯 ▮

Not too far from the locks is the *Chequers*, a Pubmaster House, where you'll receive a warm welcome.

Milton Malsor 🄯 ⊟▮ ▯

If you squint a little you can see the *Greyhound* from the canal. Children are well catered for here by a playground and games room. The beer is Theakston's with guest ales and a wide wine list; snacks and restaurant meals are always available. *The Compass* has Frog Island and John Smiths beers, but is only open in the evening during the week although all day on Saturday and Sunday when sandwiches are also available.

Rothersthorpe Locks

Attractive locks, the restored Llangollen-style liftbridge and long forgotten Osier beds are a feature of the Northampton Arm. Unfortunately the rural tranquility of the past has been destroyed by the construction of the A43 along the line of the adjacent London & North Western Railway branch line. The canal descends 107ft 10in to the Nene in a long sweeping curve, broken only by the cavernous tunnel under the M1/A43 interchange. Rothersthorpe Service Area is a short walk to the west. Just below the last Rothersthorpe lock the canal crosses a tributary of the Nene on a new aqueduct.

Bridges 9–14

The water is crystal clear below Wootton Lock and huge fish bask in the sunlight. As the canal curves round to join the Nene the Express Lifts Testing Tower looms skyward. Opened in 1982 by HM The Queen, the tower is 416ft high and contains three lift shafts. The Northampton Ring Road crosses at re-numbered Bridge 12 and Blackwood Hodge, earthmover manufacturers, have their factory by Hardingstone Lock. The canal takes on the aspect of a river as reeds and rushes press in towards the channel and weeds can be seen wafting in the clear water.

Bridge 14 – River Nene

Only the last ½ mile is less than picturesque though the massive glass and chrome Carlsberg Brewery overlooking Northampton Lock is clean and thirst provoking. Below Lock 17 BW responsibility ceases and the Environment Agency takes over. If you haven't bought a licence (see below) you may proceed only as far as the first river lock. There are good moorings along the towpath and it is only a short walk through Becketts Park to the town centre. Take care turning and beware of the weir. In times of flood you might be well advised to stay off the river and walk in to Northampton from Cotton End.

MAP 2
Northampton Arm

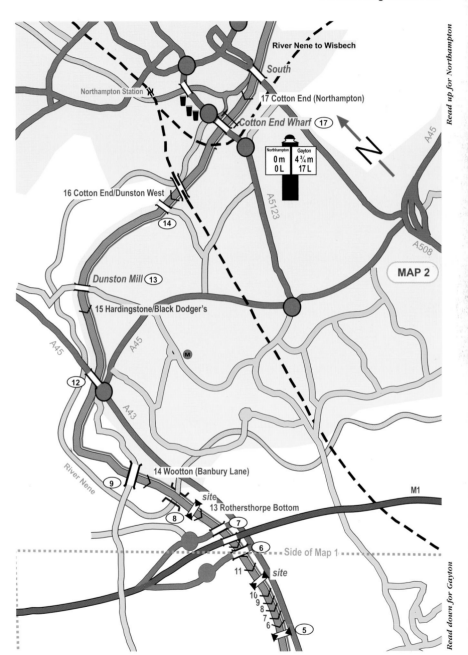

Read up for Northampton

River Nene to Wisbech

South

Northampton Station

17 Cotton End (Northampton)

Cotton End Wharf (17)

Northampton	Gayton
0 m	4 ¾ m
0 L	17 L

16 Cotton End/Dunston West

(14)

Dunston Mill (13)

15 Hardingstone/Black Dodger's

A45

A5123

A508

MAP 2

(12)

A43

A45

River Nene

14 Wootton (Banbury Lane)

(9)

site

13 Rothersthorpe Bottom

(8)

(7)

(6)

Side of Map 1

11

site

10

9

8

7

6

(5)

M1

Read down for Gayton

Northampton *All services.*

Early Closing Thurs, Principal Market Days Wed & Sat. Railway Station, Tourist Info: Mr Grant's House, St Giles Square, Northampton NN1 1DA (01604 622677, Fax 01604 604180, email: tic@ northampton.gov.uk). Daniel Defoe described Northampton as 'the handsomest and best built town in all this part of England' and though things have changed a bit since his day, the town still has a clean, prosperous air. Shoes are the main industry of Northampton and centuries of footwear have originated from tanneries built on the banks of the Nene. During the Civil War many of Cromwell's troops were shod by the townsfolk of Northampton and, in retribution, Charles II destroyed the castle and razed the town's walls to the ground. Two hundred years previously Northampton had been the setting for an earlier civil war battle between the houses of York and Lancaster. The battlefield lies near Delapre Abbey, ½mile southeast of South Bridge or south of Becketts Park. The Abbey now houses the Northants County Records Office, but the building, based on a Cluniac nunnery founded in 1145, is open in part to the public, Thurs all year, gardens every day during daylight hours, March–Sept.

Other sites of interest are:

Central Museum and Art Gallery
(Guildhall Road). This museum houses a vast collection of footwear through the ages, including a set of boots for an elephant! There are also some modern oil and water-colour paintings, ceramics and local archaeological material. Closed Christmas and New Year's Day. (01604 238548, www.northampton.gov.uk/ museums).

Hunsbury Hill Industrial Museum
(Northamptonshire Ironstone Railway Trust) (01604 702031). Cotton End. On the site of former ironstone workings and containing railway engines, wagons, and mining equipment. Exhibition of photographs and artefacts of Northants industry. Train rides. Open Easter, May–Sept Sun & Bank Hols.

Church of the Holy Sepulchre
Probably the largest and best preserved church dating from 1100 in the country.

River Nene

Navigation Authority Environment Agency, Anglian Region, Kingfisher House, Goldhay Way, Orton Goldhay, Peterborough PE2 5ZR. (01733 371811, Fax 01733 231840, www.environmental-agency.co.uk).

Licences Annual and short term licences are available. The Environment Agency and BW (see below) jointly offer a 'Gold Licence' for craft regularly using both authorities' waterways. A special key is required, however, to operate the security mechanism on the locks and this must be purchased either from local agents (who also issue permits) or by post from the Environment Agency. Once purchased, the key is usable from one year to the next. Hire boats will have to negotiate licences with their boatyard. BW at Braunston, Blisworth Tunnel Boats, The Grand Junction Boat Co and Alvechurch Boat Centres at Gayton also issue River Nene licences.

Navigation Guides The Environment Agency supply, free of charge, an excellent little booklet *Navigational Notes* covering all their waterways.
Probably the best guide to the river is the Map of the River Nene published by Imray. This includes navigation notes and distance tables as well as a detailed map.
Opus Books publish Derek Bowskill's *The Norfolk Broads and Fens*. Ordnance Survey Landranger maps 141, 142, 152 and 153 also cover the river.

Built to commemorate the First Crusade and a circular replica of the original church in Jerusalem. Includes one of the largest brasses in England. Open April–Oct, 12–5pm, key from Osborne Pawnbroker, 1 Regent Square.

Euan Corrie

Services The town centre was largely destroyed by fire in 1675 but this enabled the 17th century town planners to show their paces. The result is a magnificent Market Square, one of the largest in England, where a daily market is held. This swells on Wed and Sat to become a bustling centre of canvas-covered stalls and the source of many a bargain. On Wednesdays the emphasis is on antiques, and prices seem quite reasonable. Morrison's Supermarket is located close to the river above Northampton Lock and has cash machines. All the familiar names are represented in the town and shopping generally is excellent. There are two theatres: the Royal Theatre in Guildhall Road houses the long-established Northamptonshire Rep, in an ornate setting of gilt and red plush. (01604 624811). The Derngate Centre (Guildhall Road) hosts various exhibitions, events and entertainments through the year, (01604 626222).

Eating & Drinking Northampton's Tourist Office has a useful list of eateries ranging from American and Caribbean through Indian and Italian to tea rooms and pubs suitable for children! A walk up Bridge Street will provide the opportunity to sample every persuasion of café,

restaurant, bar, pub or estate agent! There are several large hotels in Northampton with reputable restaurants. Chinese and Indian takeaways have taken a hold in Northampton like everywhere else, but the *Plough* in Bridge Street serves more traditional dishes (ex Sun). There are countless pubs. The *Saddlers Arms*, just over South Bridge on Bridge Street serves Davenports and snacks. It might seem appropriate to try a freshly brewed Carlsberg while you are here, but opposite their plant is the *Malt Shovel*, a CAMRA pub of the year. It offers Banks', Fullers, Tetley and guest ales, Belgian bottled beers and cider, as well as displaying breweryana from Northampton's demolished Breweries. Food is available at lunchtimes except on Sundays. The *Fish Inn* in the pedestrian area offers Courage, Theakston and Marston's beers with food at lunchtime and evening. In Abington Square the *Racehorse* enjoys *Good Beer Guide* listing for its ever-changing range of beers and is open all day.

Those intent on following the first English canal built specifically as a long-distance trunk route may wish to pass by the facilities at Arm End, Gayton, and the start of the Northampton Arm which are described on page 18. But they should be cautioned that a trip down the attractive locks to Northampton and the scenic river Nene really is well worthwhile.

Gayton Junction – Bridge 51

The railway, which parallels the canal between Gayton and Whilton, crosses over south of the junction. Against the south western approach to the bridge, in the garden, can be seen traces of a large water tank, once filled by pumping from the canal, which supplied the steam locomotives as they passed over water troughs set into the tracks. The *Blisworth Hotel*, situated beside the old halt, was originally called the 'Duke of Grafton', then the 'Railway', bar snacks are available in the evenings except on Sundays and Mondays. The A43 Blisworth by-pass crosses south of bridge 48.

Blisworth ℂ ⊒ 🖥 ♿ 🍺

Ignore the modern housing and look instead at the fine brick-built warehouse of 1879, built by the Grand Junction Canal Co. Moor by Bridge 50 or 51 to visit the village. The *Royal Oak* (Courage, Hook Norton, Everard and guest beers) is welcoming and prepares lunch and evening meals every day. Games room, payphone and garden. The Post Office and General store incorporates a millstone in its steps and an off licence within as well as providing basic groceries. Open 9am–6pm, Sun 10am–12.30pm. The village newsagent opens only in the mornings. Blisworth Bridge (No 51) was also known as Candle Bridge, as the boatmen bought candles here for use in the tunnel.

Blisworth Tunnel Boats ⛺ 🚤 🛢 🅿 🛏 🎯 ♿ 🍴

(01604 858868 www.blisworthtunnel.co.uk). Hire craft (including day boats), solid fuel, boat and engine repairs, breakdowns, Boat Safety Scheme inspections, maintenance, painting and boatfitting. Wetdock and slipway. The shop stocks ice cream, souvenirs, maps, guides, chandlery and river Nene licences and keys. Brokerage is provided by Canal Craft (01604 879029/879017).

Blisworth Tunnel 3,056 yards.

Although begun in 1793 the tunnel was not completed until 1805, and then it was on a slightly revised line. William Jessop was chief engineer and originally reported that 'he had never come across ground more suitable for tunnelling'. How wrong could he be! Within two years he was so close to desperation that he was considering giving up and taking the canal over the hill with locks.

Maintenance engineers ever since have probably wished that he had, but James Barnes, the engineer directly responsible for supervising the tunnel's construction persevered and eventually completed it ten years after the rest of the canal was open. In the meantime a tramway was built to connect Blisworth and Stoke Bruerne, so that by 1800 there was a through route of sorts between

Emerging into the sunshine from the southern portal of Blisworth Tunnel.

MAP 3
Blisworth to Stoke Bruerne

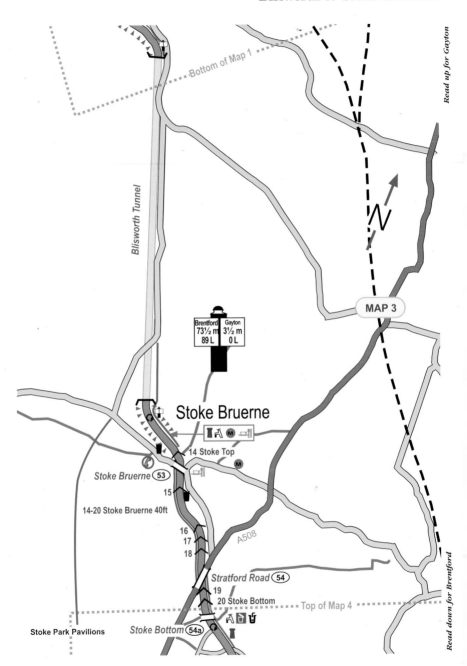

Bottom of Map 1

Read up for Gayton

Blisworth Tunnel

MAP 3

Brentford	Gayton
73½ m	3½ m
89 L	0 L

Stoke Bruerne

14 Stoke Top

Stoke Bruerne (53)

15

14-20 Stoke Bruerne 40ft

16
17
18

A508

Stratford Road (54)

19
20 Stoke Bottom

Top of Map 4

Stoke Park Pavilions

Stoke Bottom (54a)

Read down for Brentford

Birmingham and London. Most surprisingly, considering its length and all the problems, the tunnel is straight. There is no towpath and for 66 years boats had to be legged through while horses were walked over the top. The path is now a minor road and easy to follow.

Legging was notoriously dangerous and many men died before tugs were introduced in 1871. Trains of as many as 25 boats were known to have been towed through by a single tug, which meant it could have reached Blisworth Mill before the last boat came out! Another quite remarkable statistic is contained in the statement by a Mr Clarke in 1912, that he had been working the tug for 24 years, and had an estimated 69,936 trips through as tug master. Accepting 45 mins per journey this means that he spent 6 years inside the tunnel! (We are indebted to Mr Ken Sherwood for collecting these details). The tugs were retired in 1936, though winding holes, sheds and moorings at either end remain to provide evidence of their work.

In recent years Blisworth Tunnel has been continually plagued by repair closures, the most recent stretching almost without break for over 4 years. Remedial work at a cost of some £4.5m, including the complete re-lining of the central third was carried out in 1983/84.

There is no towpath and canoes are prohibited. Boats must, of course, be equipped with a headlight.

Stoke Bruerne ▮ 🄲

Stoke Bruerne was chosen to become the site for Britain's first canal museum even before commercial traffic had finished and BW took over from British Transport Waterways. For many years the late Jack James had been winning awards for his efforts in maintaining the locks at Stoke Bruerne, and his display of traditional canal ware in the old leggers' hut was always much admired. When Jack won yet again in 1961 the BTW General Manager, hearing of the award, decided that the old mill at Stoke Bruerne was the best place for the museum. The district engineer at

the time was Charles Hadlow and he joined forces with Jack James in collecting material. The museum opened on 4th May 1963 and, by the time it 'came of age' in 1984, over one million visitors had passed through its doors.

The Canal Museum ▮ 🄰 ⌁ 🄰

contains countless artefacts from the commercial days of boating, including engines, painted ware, china, clothing and hundreds of photographs. Larger exhibits include working boats outside the door and the replica of butty boat *Sunny Valley's* cabin inside.

An exhibit not always connected with the museum itself is the boat weighing machine installed in the duplicate top lock outside. This was built for the Glamorganshire Canal in 1834 and was capable of weighing boats of up to 40 tons. It had fallen into disuse by 1914 and was presented to the BTW in 1955. It was moved from its original site near Cardiff Castle and installed at Stoke Bruerne in 1963. It now holds a 'station boat' built for work on Birmingham's canals.

The museum includes an excellent canal shop, with quite the best stock of canal books you will find anywhere. As befits its location, the shop sells canal ware.

The museum opening times are: summer (Easter to October) 10am–5pm, winter (October to Easter) Tues–Sun 10am–4pm. Last admission ½hr before closing. Special rates for party and school bookings. Enquiries: The Curator, The Canal Museum, Stoke Bruerne, Towcester, Northants (01604 862229, www. thewaterwaystrust.co.uk).

A useful 'Historical Trail' pamphlet describing the village is available from the Canal Museum, price 10p, and using this it is possible to discover a great deal more about the village.

Rookery Open Farm Museum up Rookery Lane towards Roade, offers the chance of hands-on encounters with lambs, calves, waterfowl, goats and other inhabitants as well as a tea room. It is open daily Mar–Oct (01604 864885).

There's always plenty of activity at the top of Stoke Bruerne Locks. Visitors watch boats start their descent to the Tove Valley whilst working boats are tied up outside the museum in the right background.

A travelling shop visits the village on Wed and Fri mornings at about 9am. It is possible to order newspapers by arrangement with Andrew Woodward at *The Boat Inn*, to whom they are delivered each morning. On Mondays a fish & chip van calls outside *The Boat Inn* at about 9pm. Other provisions are available from the *Boat*. There is no longer a Post Office in Stoke Bruerne, but the postmaster calls at the village hall on Tuesday mornings 10am–noon to dispense pensions and stamps. The Bruerne's Lock shop by the top lock sells ice cream and cold drinks every day except Monday, May–Sept.

Eating and Drinking There are three restaurants: *Bruerne's Lock* next to the lock features in the *Good Food Guide*. It is a small, intimate, but busy restaurant whose menu takes full advantage of some excellent local produce. Booking is essential (01604 863654). On the opposite side of the canal is the famous *Boat Inn*. There are three parts to the pub. The bar serves Mansfield, Frog Island, Banks and Adnams beers, with bar snacks available. Throughout the day the bar snack menu

and ice creams are available in the Bistro next door. Open daily throughout the year (9.30am–6pm), except for winter Monday lunches), home-made pies, puddings, cakes & scones feature on the menu. *The Boat* also has a full a la carte restaurant, booking is advised (01604 862428).

Adjacent to the museum is *The Old Chapel Restaurant & Coffee House*, which keeps an interesting selection of crafts and gifts as well as providing beers and wines, hot and cold drinks, home made bread, soups and cream teas – all cooked to order. It is open Tues–Sun 10am–5pm in summer and Wed–Sun 10am–dusk in winter.

Mrs Blagrove in *Wharf Cottage* offers Bed & Breakfast, with rooms overlooking the canal. (01604 862174). Her husband, David, is a well-known canal historian and will give guided tours of the area and arrange special excursion weekends (01604 862174).

In addition to the main shop in the museum there are others on the canal front. The Canal Shop beside Wharf Cottage sells ropework fenders, painted ware and gifts.

Boat Trips Two small boats run regular trips along the canal through Stoke Bruerne. The *Indian Chief*, based at *The Boat Inn*, runs public trips to the tunnel on weekend afternoons Mar–Sept. Details: 01604 862428.

Stoke Bruerne Boat Co (01604 862107) offers trips to Blisworth Tunnel aboard the 30-seat *Charlie* and has 12-seater self steer day boat *Skylark* for hire.

J & M Canal Carriers 🛢 The Wharf, Stoke Bruerne. (07966 503609). Coal and carrying charter. Members of the Commercial Boat Operators Association.

Stoke Park Pavilions When completed in 1635 Stoke Park was the earliest Palladian style building in England. Built by Inigo Jones, the house has since been demolished, but pavilions, a colonnade and the fine gardens remain. Open occasionally in high summer.

Stoke Bruerne Locks

A seven-lock flight separates the 16 mile 'Blisworth Pound' from the 6 mile 'Stoke Pound' to Cosgrove. In the 1830s all the locks between Stoke Bruerne and Marsworth were duplicated to speed traffic and save water, only to be filled in 20 years later when trade began to decline. The original top lock was excavated in the early 1960s to site the boat-weighing machine moved from Cardiff. The iron bottom gates came from Welshpool Town Lock on the Montgomery Canal, and are rather unusual, being curved and having round balance beams.

A more recent addition to the village is *The Navigation* alongside the second lock, which is open all day every day for Marstons, Mansfield, and Banks beers with bar meals and indoor and outdoor play areas for children.

The site of an old brickworks can be seen below lock 15, together with its wharf. The cottage at lock 16, boasts an attractive Italianesque bay window, while the line of the old tramway can be seen rising up the east side of the flight. This was used before completion of Blisworth

Tunnel to connect the finished canal at Blisworth with that below Stoke Bruerne locks. Alongside lock 19 is hard standing where carrying boats can be loaded.

Stoke Bruerne Bottom Lock

🍴 🏕 ⛴ 🅱 Together with its ivy-clad cottages this is a picturesque lock, with the original course of the river Tove entering just below. Since the canal was built, this confluence has been a busy site, initially with wharves, basins and working boats, but today is a useful source of private moorings. A pump-house draws water up to the summit pound in times of low water.

Below Stoke Locks a series of handsome brick arches carries the towpath over a pair of weirs which fall away to the Tove, now passing beneath the canal in a culvert. Pumps here can be used to augment canal water supplies from the river with the water being pumped uphill around Stoke and Buckby Locks, if required. The land rises gently towards Grafton Regis in the west and the lofty 15th century spire of Hanslope's Norman church can be seen to the east.

Grafton Regis 🍴 🅲

The large church is a combination of Norman and 15th century (key from 'Millstones', Bozenham Mill Lane, Grafton Regis) and contains a fine rood screen, a monument by Flaxman, and Woodville tombs. Nearby, a medieval manor house destroyed during the Civil War was the home of Elizabeth Woodville, mother of the Princes in the Tower who were reputedly murdered by Richard III. The *White Hart* (01908 542123), which is closed on Mondays, is a Greene King pub serving bar meals that are individually prepared by the owner-chef (ex Sunday) and playing Northants skittles and other pub games (no dogs).

Yardley Gobion 🅱 🍴 🅲 🍺 🅱

Early Closing Wed. From Yardley Wharf it's a short walk up to the village, though take care on the busy road. The imposing

MAP 4
Stoke Bruerne to Yardley Gobion

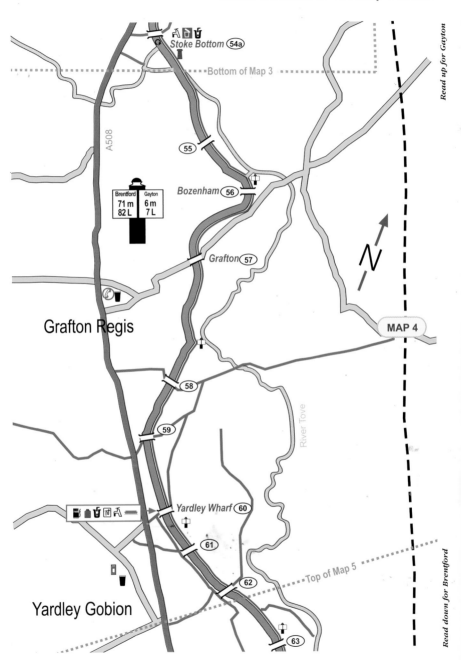

Stoke Bottom (54a)

Bottom of Map 3

A508

55

Brentford	Gayton
71 m	6 m
82 L	7 L

Bozenham 56

Grafton 57

Grafton Regis

58

59

Yardley Wharf 60

61

River Tove

Yardley Gobion

62

Top of Map 5

63

MAP 4

Read up for Gayton

Read down for Brentford

Georgian house with attendant bell tower visible from the canal, is Yardley House. The *Coffee Pot Tavern* (01908 542106) is an Enterprise Inn serving meals. There's a garden and payphone, and children are welcome if they're eating. There's a small Post Office and Costcutter Supermarket in the housing estate beyond the village centre.

Kingfisher Marina
Yardley Gobion Wharf (01908 542293) Full Boatyard services are available as described below. John and Susie Bowen also offer very comfortable self-catering and B&B accommodation at the restored wharf (Tourist Board Approved).

Baxter Boatfitting Services (01908 542844) are also at Yardley Gobion Wharf providing boatyard services including chandlery and slipway, breakdown cover, repairs, steelwork, cranage and solid fuel.

Bridges 60–64

Pasture land falls away eastwards towards the banks of the Tove, pheasants strut across the fields and herons seem conspicuously common.

Castlethorpe

The village itself is 1 mile east. There's a pub, the *Carrington Arms*, serving

Greene King beers and with skittles and pool to play. The small but comprehensive Post Office/General Store, will deliver larger orders and stocks gas and solid fuels. Castlethorpe has the remains of a motte and bailey castle. By Bridge 64 is the *Navigation Inn* (01908 543156), a free house in the old tradition. Greene King and regularly changing guest beers are served. Food is always available and there's a garden, payphone, children's room, canalside bar, plus a short slipway and mooring for patrons. The landlord has worked hard to produce a warm and friendly canalside pub in the old tradition.

Cosgrove

recycling bins. A village displaying an interesting architectural mix. Cosgrove Hall is an early 18th century bay-fronted building with grounds down to the canal. Cosgrove Priory, discernible through trees to the east now comprises office accommodation. The church was modernised in Victorian times, but the weathercock is genuine 14th century. The *Barley Mow* is a popular pub, open all day, welcoming locals, boaters and fishermen alike. The home-cooked food is excellent . . . especially the traditional Sunday lunch. Bar

Mellow stone at Cosgrove Ornamental Bridge.

Euan Corrie

MAP 5
Yardley to Wolverton

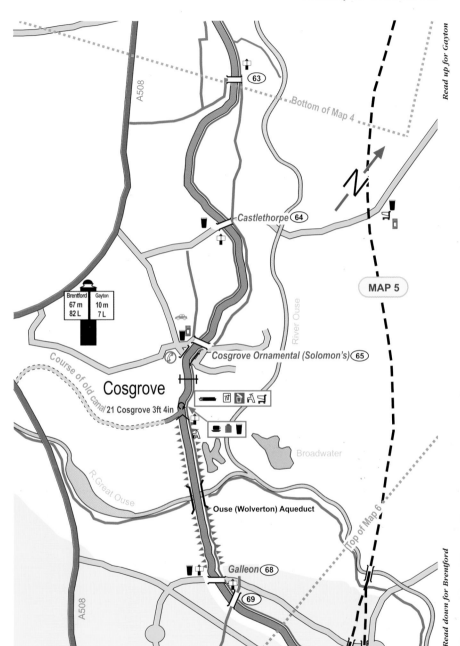

Read up for Gayton

63

Bottom of Map 4

A508

Castlethorpe 64

MAP 5

River Ouse

	Brentford	Gayton
	67 m	10 m
	82 L	7 L

Course of old canal

Cosgrove Ornamental (Solomon's) 65

Cosgrove

21 Cosgrove 3ft 4in

Broadwater

R.Great Ouse

Ouse (Wolverton) Aqueduct

[Top of Map 6]

Galleon 68

69

A508

Read down for Brentford

meals are available every day. Beers are from Courage and John Smiths with additional changing guests. Crossing the canal is the unusual Gothic form of Solomon's Bridge. Built in 1800 there appears to be no real reason for its unique design. Similarly eccentric is the narrow underpass which threads a footpath under the canal to link Cosgrove village with The Green. Here is the *New Cosgrove Lodge Hotel*, a free house. The adjacent Cosgrove Leisure Park caravan site (01908 563360) is set in 110 acres of parkland and boasts 7 lakes, a café, swimming and shop (open 9.30am–2.30pm, Mon–Fri, 8am–7pm weekends, but longer in summer) and sells Calor Gas and fish & chips.

Stratford & Buckingham Canal

Only the first few yards of this branch remain in water and are used for moorings, while further on the canal passes through a bird sanctuary. Originally, when the branch was opened to Buckingham in 1801 it was 10½ miles long and had two locks. Agriculturally motivated, the principal traffic was hay and straw for carriage to London, where horse fodder was in short supply. Surprisingly, boatbuilding became important in later years, with the famous Edward Hayes yard at Old Stratford (public house, Post Office/general store 1½ miles). Most unusual was the dominance of sea-going and harbour vessels built there, rather than the canal boats one might expect. Founded in 1840, steam launches, tugs and riverboats were built for more than 80 years, many of the smaller vessels making their own way to London by canal while larger craft had to be transhipped in sections and re-assembled. The site, beside the old A5, is now a garage. When the yard closed in 1928 the canal to Buckingham was already near to dereliction, but the widening and lowering of the old A5 caused the abandonment of the Stratford–Buckingham length in 1961. The first 1½

miles remained however, offering tempting opportunities for restoration, which is promoted by an enthusiastic society despite the fact that a typically short-sighted local authority levelled the few remaining bridges several years ago.

Linda Cruising Co Cosgrove Lock. (01604 861911). Public trips and private charter aboard 40-seat *Elizabeth of Glamis*. Catering available on charter trips if required, on board bar with draught beer and real ales.

Cosgrove Marina Cosgrove Lock (01908 562467). Moorings, repairs, maintenance & breakdown, hard standing and brokerage. Fishing permits and day tickets for 'Broadwaters'.

The Great Ouse, or Wolverton, Aqueduct

When the canal opened it crossed the Ouse on the level, descending into the valley via a series of nine locks, five to the north, four to the south. It soon became clear that this would pose problems, both in terms of time wasted and also during periods of flood when the river couldn't be crossed at all. In 1805 William Jessop built an aqueduct, which collapsed in 1808. A temporary wooden trough was then set up using what remained of Jessop's work as a base. In 1811 Benjamin Bevan came up with the design in cast iron consisting of wedge-shaped plates within a series of arched ribs. It worked.

Great Ouse and the Bedford–Milton Keynes Link

In 1981 a plan was announced to rebuild the locks down to the river and re-open the Great Ouse to navigation from Bedford, so linking with the Fenland waterways.

With the Great Ouse now open to navigation upstream to Kempstone Mill, above Bedford, this plan has now developed onto one for a largely new navigation with a number of potential routes which will be incorporated into redevelopment of former brickworks. Full details and information about membership of the Bedford &

Crossing the Great Ouse at Wolverton Aqueduct. The temporary crossing reached by locks down the valley side, in use between 1800 and 1811, was in the foreground. This was initially replaced by a three-arched brick aqueduct, which collapsed in 1808; its foundations may be seen on the river bed.

Milton Keynes Waterway Trust are available from The Gables, Broughton, Milton Keynes MK10 9AA (www.b-mkwaterway. org.uk).

Old Wolverton

A victim of the Enclosure Acts, relatively little remains of the village except ridges and bumps in the ground ½mile southwest of Bridge 68 or others round the farm ¼ mile east. You may even be able to distinguish the mound of the Norman Castle, but don't be deceived by the church – it's less than 200 years old. The *Galleon* (open all day Fri–Sun) serves Youngs, Old Speckled Hen and London Pride. Home made food is available Tue–Thur lunch & eve and all day Fri–Sun and there's a beer garden, complete with duplicate 28 mile post, and moorings.

Bridges 68–71

Leaving the Ouse embankment the canal passes through a shallow cutting before facing the factories and chimneys of Wolverton. The area suffers somewhat from graffiti and litter and, for those heading south is a rather uncharacteristic introduction to Milton Keynes.

Wolverton *All services, Early Closing Wed, Market Day Fri.* The services are useful and there's good access to the town centre and station. An information board beneath Bridge 71 may help those intent on exploration. The town is best known for the BR Carriage & Wagon Works to the south of the canal, where the Queen's carriage was built. Half a mile south of the shops is the Milton Keynes Museum (01908 316222, www.mkmuseum.

org.uk), which is entered from McConnell Drive. An interesting exhibition of the area's past, this is a 'working' museum, with many active demonstrations. It includes a fascinating 'hands on' display of telephone and telecommunications equipment, a Stony Stratford tramcar and hosts regularly changing displays and demonstrations. Open (Easter–October) Wed–Sun but only at weekends in winter. (If you come across some concrete cows you've gone too far!)

Bridge 71 – New Bradwell

Crossing a new aqueduct the canal rounds new housing and flooded former gravel pits to arrive at New Bradwell. Overseeing all is the famous sandstone windmill built by Samuel Holman in 1816. Used until 1871 for grinding corn, it has been restored to working condition and is open summer Sunday afternoons (01908 315428).

By Bridge 72 is the *New Inn* (01908 312094), a Charles Wells pub, open all day, with a restaurant and serving bar meals every lunch & all but Sunday eve. There are moorings, pool table, payphone, a beer garden. Walking north leads to useful shops, takeaways and two more Charles Wells' pubs: The *Foresters Arms* and the *Cuba*.

Great Linford ▌ Ⓒⴹ⬚ⵗ ⬸⬛

Between New Bradwell and Great Linford the canal swings out beyond Milton Keynes to pass briefly through open countryside once more.

The river Ouse, now in league with the Tove, spreads out to flood gravel workings in the valley below. Part of Stantonbury Lake is a wildlife sanctuary (closed to the public) and others are noted for coarse fishing. The once-historic *Black Horse* by Bridge 76 has become a member of the Vintage Inns chain as *The Proud Perch*. It has been much refurbished but still offers moorings and has a welcoming atmosphere being open all day. The beer is Tetley, Bass and Guinness. Refurbishment has provided a galleried eating area – servery and bar food is always available (01908 605939) and families are welcome. There are also a payphone and garden. Bus services to central Milton Keynes. The village itself is best approached from the new wharf or Bridge 77. Like many villages swallowed up by Milton Keynes, the planners have retained what they could and the centre is little changed. The restored almshouses were refurbished in 1975. The Arts Centre (01908 608108, www. artworks-mk.co.uk) holds exhibitions and concerts and the courtyard houses pottery, jewellery, silversmithing and other workshops. A few minutes walk will take you to the local centre at St Ledger Court with its Co-Op, Post Office and takeaway. The thatched *Nags Head* has changing guest ales and serves lunches (ex Sun), and has a payphone, but does not allow dogs or children.

Newport Pagnell Branch

This wasn't a failure but its life was short. In 1863 it sold out to the Newport Pagnell Railway who built their line over much of its length. It left the Grand Junction just by Bridge 77 where a workshop is now sited (Unigas). The railway too has gone and now forms part of the Redway walk system.

Bridges 77–79

An area where the Milton Keynes we have been led to expect shows its face, though the boxlike houses are viewed across tended parkland and playing fields. Bridge 78 has been totally rebuilt but plans for a short canal arm to a local community shopping centre have come to nothing. There are, however, water, elsan & rubbish disposal facilities and moorings for boaters at Bridge 78 alongside the *Gifford Park*, which has a patio, play area, family lounge and dining room and serves Whitbread ales and meals all day, every day. Across the road are useful shops, including a Post Office, general store/off licence and fish & chip shop.

MAP 6
Wolverton to Great Linford

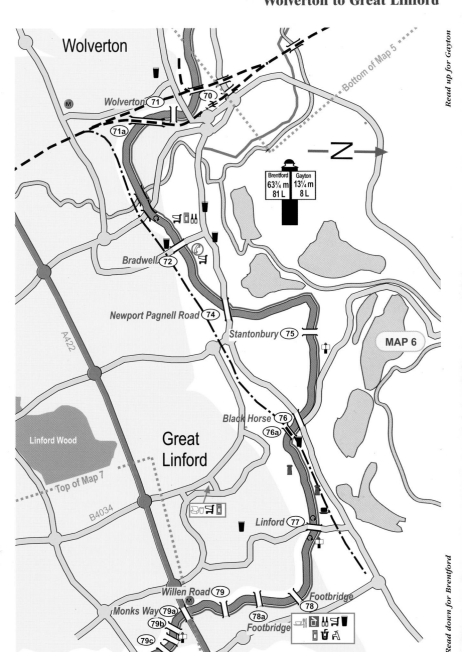

Wolverton

Bottom of Map 5

Read up for Gayton

Wolverton 71

70

71a

N

Brentford	Gayton
63¾ m	13¼ m
81 L	8 L

Bradwell 72

Newport Pagnell Road 74

Stantonbury 75

MAP 6

A422

Black Horse 76

76a

Linford Wood

Great
Linford

Top of Map 7

B4034

Linford 77

Willen Road 79

Footbridge

Monks Way 79a

78

79b

78a

79c

Footbridge

Robin Smithett

Close to Bridge 79 are Great Linford (or The Dell) Brickworks which were in use from the late 1800s to about 1911 and were restored in the 1980s.

Milton Keynes *All Services, Tourist Info: Margaret Powell Square, 890 Midsummer Boulevard, Central Milton Keynes, Buckinghamshire MK9 3QA (0870 1201269, Fax 01908 558315, www.imk.co.uk) A&E at Milton Keynes Central Hospital on Standing Way near Bridge 88/Milton Keynes Marina but always dial 999 first in an emergency.*

Ignore the warnings and the slanderous comments. If only all canalside towns were such a pleasure to boat through! (Or even appreciated their canal half as much.) It takes almost a day to pass through but is neither tedious nor unattractive. Conceived in the 1960s, the city was (and is) something novel in new towns. There was nothing here before, just fields and a village called Milton Keynes. The village is still there, surprisingly unchanged (1 mile west of Bridge 83) but the rest has altered beyond all recognition. 22,000 acres were earmarked in 1967, work started in the early 70s and since then houses have been built and a population of 100,000 plus has developed. The houses may not be to everyone's taste but the main shopping centre

is acknowledged as one of the largest and best in Europe. One of the advantages of the extensive development has been the chance to investigate local archeological and industrial remains and many of the resulting preserved sites are described in leaflets available from the Visitor Information Centre or can be visited on guided walks. (0870 1201269, www.mkweb.co.uk)

(Shopping Information: 0845 6806688). Moor near Childs Way and walk (¾ mile west) or catch the bus.

Pennylands Marina A 6½ acre development of luxury houses and flats with private moorings.

Willen Lake & Park Peeping over the ridge behind Newlands Park is the Buddhist Peace Pagoda, first in the western hemisphere. This shares the view over Willen Lake with the church of St Mary Magdalene, reputedly the only Wren church outside London. The lake is a water sports centre complete with fountain.

Woolstone ▮ ⓒ 🍴 🗋 ⚭ ⌂

In Woolstone the *Barge Inn*, one of the Vintage Inns group, is open all day. Beer is Bass and Tetley and hot meals are served from the Pantry. There is a garden. West of the canal is a 'Local Centre'.

Milton Keynes Marina ▬ ▮ 🏕 📷 ▮

🗋 ▮ 🐕 At Peartree Bridge (88). Apart from the timeshare craft, Lockhart Marine (01908 672672, email lockhart-marine@btconnect.com) provide the services, workshop, repairs & servicing, slipway with 72ft cradle, chandlery, moorings, outboard sales & servicing, Boat Safety Scheme Inspections, breakdowns, boat building, repairs and painting, sales & brokerage, gifts, books, maps & guides. Closed Monday.

Woughton on the Green ⚭ 🍴 ▮

Centred round a huge open green. this is a pretty village. The *Old Swan* prefers to be known as "a pub that does food" and prioritises on Courage and Moreland beers with guest ales but it specialises in

MAP 7
Milton Keynes

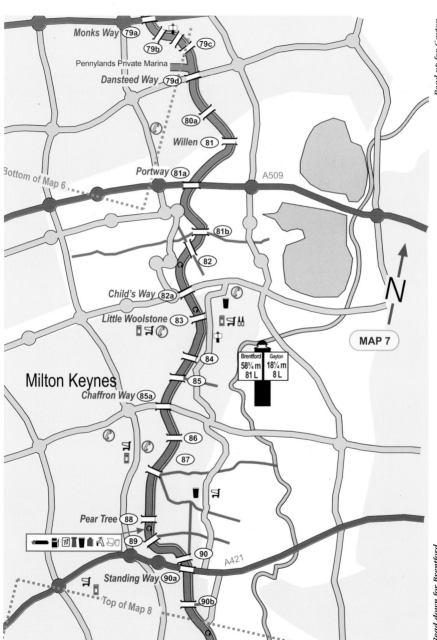

Robin Smitbett

Fenny Stratford with its shallow lock, swing bridge and pub presents a tranquil scene close to the heart of Milton Keynes.

traditional English cooking and really is old. It is open and serves food all day every day. There is a useful general store/off licence opposite.

The Open University is sited ¾ mile east of Bridge 90 at Walton Hall.

Simpson 🍺 ©

Now that the A4146 has been diverted away from the heart of Simpson, the waterborne visitor can remain aloof on the embankment above. The *Plough* has a canalside garden, and access to the village is good from the towpath. The pub (Charles Wells) provides lunches, dinners and bar snacks (ex Sun eve). Booking is advised for Sunday lunch, vegetarians are catered for and the pub is open all day at weekends. Simpson Wharf has been thoughtfully renovated and is now part of the nearby 'George Amey Outdoor Activities Centre' for the Bucks Association of Boys Clubs.

Bridges 91–95

The canal twists under the old main road to encounter some light industry. Beside

Bletchley Timber Yard is Sophie Miller's Fenny Lodge Art Gallery, where there are paintings, prints including canal prints, ceramics and jewellery.

Fenny Stratford Lock 🏕 ⚓

🔋 🍴 This rather feeble lock was necessary because the section north just wouldn't hold water at first. Building the lock in June 1802 and dropping the level solved the problem. The lock is unusual in having a swing bridge spanning the chamber, though this rarely moves nowadays. Overlooking is the *Red Lion*, a Carlsberg-Tetley pub.

Fenny Stratford & Bletchley

All services, Early Closing Wed Bletchley Market Day Thurs & Sat. Quite where one ends and the other begins only the planners know. Bletchley's role in Milton Keynes is that of 'workshop', while Fenny Stratford has more to offer the boater, with useful shops, several comfortable pubs and an interesting habit of letting off canon in the churchyard on November 11th. These 'Fenny Poppers' celebrate the church's

MAP 8
Milton Keynes to Bletchley

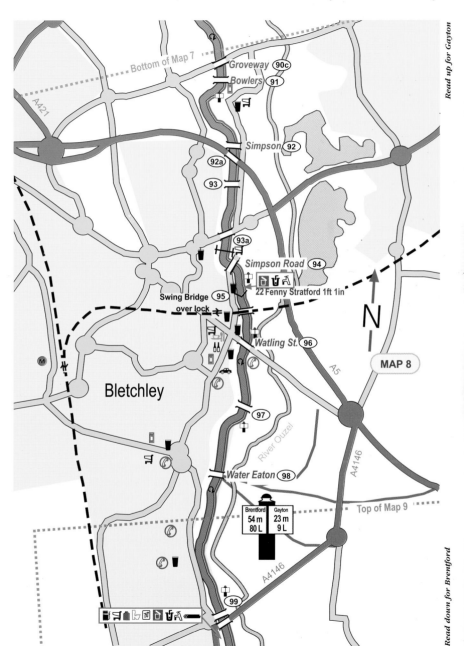

Read up for Gayton

Bottom of Map 7

A421

Groveway (90c)

Bowlers (91)

Simpson (92)

(92a)

(93)

(93a)

Simpson Road (94)

22 Fenny Stratford 1ft 1in

Swing Bridge over lock (95)

Watling St. (96)

Bletchley

MAP 8

N

A5

(97)

Water Eaton (98)

River Ouzel

Top of Map 9

A4146

Brentford	Gayton
54 m	23 m
80 L	9 L

A4146

(99)

Read down for Brentford

founding in 1730 by Dr. Browne Willis. The main road is quieter now that the A5 bypasses the centre but it still carries some heavy lorries. Among the pubs, the *Swan,* which is open all day, has a range of snacks at the bar (Mon–Sat) and Adnams and Tetley beers. Other facilities include Indian and Chinese takeaways, fish & chips and an ironmonger stocking Calor Gas. Nearby is the Bletchley Leisure Centre, with swimming pool and catering facilities.

At Fenny Stratford, Woughton and Wolverton are signboards erected jointly by the Southeast region of the Association of Waterway Cruising Clubs, British Waterways and the Milton Keynes Development Corporation. They consist of a map and local details useful to those wishing to explore Milton Keynes more thoroughly.

Bridges 96–99

Fenny Stratford hides Bletchley to the west, while Milton Keynes Football Club lies east. The river Ouzel is evident here and the canal crosses a tributary on a small aqueduct near Waterhall Park, a designated picnic and 'kickabout' area. Though the official Milton Keynes boundary crosses at Bridge 99, a more rural border exists at Bridge 98. The *Plough* (west of Bridge 98) offers Carlsberg–Tetley beers, discos on Fri and Sat and a big screen TV for football. It is open all day and there is a PO and shops opposite.

Those undeterred by a mile and a half's walk can reach Bletchley Park (just beyond the station from Bridge 98) where code breakers made valuable but unseen contributions to Allied knowledge of German intentions during World War II. In addition to code-breaking equipment, displays cover the earliest computers, Churchill and wartime memorabilia. Bletchley Park Museum is open every weekend from March to mid-December. (www.bletchley-park.org.uk 01908 640404).

Willowbridge Marina (01908 643242). Repairs &

maintenance, boatfitting & steelwork, cranage, moorings, toilets, showers, laundry, coal. The shop is open every day and sells chandlery, guides, postcards & stamps, provisions, ice cream and hot pies.

Nationwide Narrowboats 86 Wingfield Road, Tebworth, Bedfordshire LU7 9QQ (01525 874335, www.canaljunction.com/ nationwide) offers hire craft from Willowbridge Marina, which may be chartered for longer term cruising.

APS (01908 376932) Ray Ayres is based at Willowbridge Marina and will attend to engine & boat repairs and breakdowns.

Scott Welding & Fabrication (0777 0416933) build narrowboats and barges specifically to individual order at Willowbridge Marina.

Bridge 102 – Soulbury Locks

A 5-mile trek away over the rolling uplands of Bedfordshire is Woburn Abbey. Home of the Dukes of Bedford, the house boasts many priceless art treasures (21 Canalettos!) gardens, a pottery, antique centre, restaurants (enquiries: 01525 290666, www.woburnabbey.co.uk) and wildlife reserve (01525 290407, www.woburnsafari.co.uk). To get there from the canal, follow signs for Gt Brickhill, Lt Brickhill and Woburn, otherwise catch a bus from Stratford or Leighton Buzzard. The side ponds at Stoke Hammond Lock are inoperable and the swing bridge (105) isn't about to work either. A slight cutting marks the approaches of Soulbury Locks.

Stoke Hammond

Early Closing Sat. Free of Milton Keynes and marking a brief respite in the locks from London, Stoke Hammond is worthy of a breather. Five minutes from Bridge 106 brings you to the *Dolphin* a friendly local pub serving Adnams and bar meals. There's a beer garden with ducks.

Three Locks

The old working boat people insisted the locks were haunted by a woman and her

MAP 9
Bletchley to Soulbury

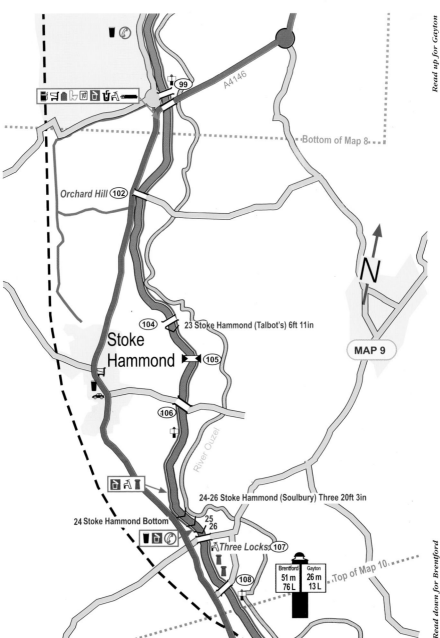

Read up for Gayton

(99)

A4146

Bottom of Map 8

Orchard Hill (102)

N

MAP 9

(104) 23 Stoke Hammond (Talbot's) 6ft 11in

Stoke Hammond

(105)

(106)

River Ouzel

24-26 Stoke Hammond (Soulbury) Three 20ft 3in

24 Stoke Hammond Bottom

25
26

Three Locks (107)

Brentford	Gayton
51 m	26 m
76 L	13 L

Top of Map 10

(108)

Read down for Brentford

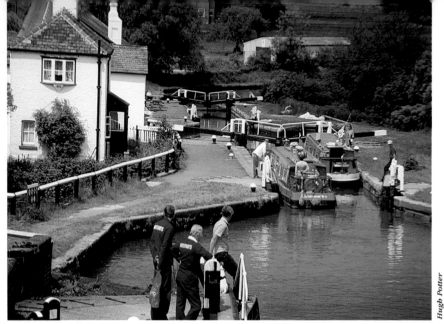

The close spacing of the three locks at Soulbury make it even more important to fill the one below before opening paddles further up the flight if embarrassing towpath floods and waste of water are to be avoided.

baby – on a still night you may hear the squeak of pram wheels as she walks by. The *Three Locks* pub, always popular, does bar food all day in summer and every lunch & eve in winter. There's a 'pick-your-own' fruit farm just to the east of the locks.

Note: With short pounds, side ponds that don't always work and so much distraction it's easy to waste water. Check for oncoming boats who might make better use of water levels, share locks and, if heading down, ensure that the lock below is full before emptying yours.

The working boatmen knew Soulbury Locks as "Stoke Hammond Three" and the pound between them and Leighton as "Jackdaw Pound".

Soulbury ⊟▮ ⓒ ▯

One mile SW of Bridge 107, there's a bookshop cum antique shop on the way and a pleasant walk to justify the excursion.

Bridge 107–112

Gently rolling farmland is dotted with the occasional mill and farm buildings, and the canal forms a three-quarter moat around Old Linslade. The *Globe* is a quaint old pub with a canalside terrace, moorings and play area. Recently refurbished, it offers restaurant food all day every day, plus afternoon teas at weekends (book evenings and weekends 01525 373338) beers include Abbott, Greene King, Ruddles and guests. Passing through Bridge 112 (open) leads to picturesque Leighton Lock, highlighted by neat lawns, overhanging trees and whitewashed walls.

Wyvern Shipping Co Ltd ▬ ▬ 🅰 🏧 ▮
▮ (01525 372355, www.canalholidays. co.uk). Boat hire, boat building, fitting, painting, repairs & maintenance, covered boat building, moorings. Established in 1954, the yard is open weekdays all year, plus Saturdays April to October inclusive.

Leighton Lady (01525 384563, www.leightonlady.freeuk.com). Canalside at Brantom's Wharf, Leighton Bridge. Public and charter trips aboard 54-seat passenger narrowboat and day boat hire.

MAP 10
Linslade and Leighton

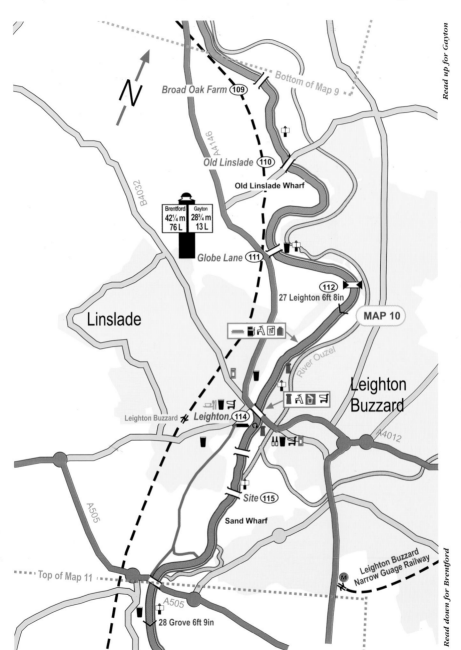

Read up for Gayton

Bottom of Map 9

Broad Oak Farm (109)

A4146

Old Linslade (110)

Old Linslade Wharf

Brentford	Gayton
42¼ m	28¾ m
76 L	13 L

B4032

Globe Lane (111)

(112)

27 Leighton 6ft 8in

MAP 10

Linslade

River Ouzel

Leighton
Buzzard

A4012

Leighton Buzzard ⚞ Leighton (114)

Site (115)

Sand Wharf

A505

Leighton Buzzard
Narrow Guage Railway

Top of Map 11

A505

28 Grove 6ft 9in

Read down for Brentford

Linslade *Most services* 🏕 ⛽ 📱 🛒

Historically the Ouzel kept Linslade and Leighton apart, though the canal provides a more obvious boundary today. Just up the hill from Bridge 114 is a kebab house. Also nearby is the *Bedford Arms*, a pub with B&B accommodation preparing lunchtime and evening meals Mon–Sat as well as Sunday lunches. Alternatively in Church Road is the *Hunt Hotel* offering Bass, Fuller or Tetley beers and meals at lunchtime and in the evening, except on Sundays. There is also an Indian restaurant and takeaways offering kebabs, Indian or Chinese food. Canalside is a large Tesco supermarket.

Leighton Buzzard *All services, Market Day Tue and Sat and Farmers' Market on the 3rd Sat each month, Early Closing Thurs.*

Visitor moorings are strictly controlled and are limited to 14 days. Longer stays may be negotiated with the moorings warden who lives aboard his boat by Bridge 114. With Linslade this is now considered as one town. Leighton Buzzard is a large and pleasant market town with several interesting buildings, ranging from quaint timber-and-brick thatched cottages to modern office blocks. Shops including Tesco are only moments away from Bridge 114. You won't see the town at its best until you find the Market Square – note the Market House of 1852, later converted to the Fire Station. The Cross dates from 1400 and beside the PO is the even older *Golden Bells Inn*. The *Black Lion* serves Benskins all day every day as well as offering bar meals. Head up North Street to see Holly Lodge, a handsome 17th century brick house, and the Wilkes Almshouses.

There are ample opportunities to eat out in Leighton Buzzard but we can recommend the excellent value bar meals served at the *Roebuck,* just off the Market Square. A Waitrose supermarket is hidden just off the High Street.

Leighton Buzzard Narrow Gauge Railway (01525 373888, www.buzzrail. co.uk) runs from Pages Park (by the A4146) through a varied townscape and out into open countryside. Using historic steam locomotives the railway offers a real family outing and a distinct change from boating. It operates on Sunday (Mar–Oct), Wednesday as well in July, all except Mon & Fri in August and on Bank Holidays and the station and shop remain open on winter Sundays.

Bridges 114–120

The disused Linslade–Dunstable railway line serves as a footpath. The disused and infilled pits just here and several old wharves bear witness to the canal traffic generated by the George Garside Sand & Gravel works, some still showing relics of the narrow gauge railways which served them. To the east the mellow-coloured steeple and high spire of All Saints church towers high over squat St Mary's, Linslade to the west. The river is companion to the canal between Slapton and Milton Keynes. Grove lock house has been swamped in its conversion to The *Grove Lock* pub (01525 380940), which serves meals every day including roast Sunday lunches and Fullers Beers. On the lockside is an original Grand Junction milestone: '45 miles to the Thames'.

Church Lock has a tiny 14th century chapel, now converted to a private house, and at Slapton Lock it is easy to see the infilled duplicate lock of 1830.

Slapton 🍴 🎣

A brisk stroll to Slapton is amply rewarded. The *Carpenter's Arms* is very old, but recently refurbished. It has a garden and serves Vale Brewery Ales, guest beers, and home cooked food every lunch and eve (you'll need to book at weekends: 01525 220563).

Bridges 121–123

This is a remote section marked only by a succession of isolated locks. The building beside Bridge 123, now a private house, was once the *Brownlow Arms*.

MAP 11
Grove to Ivinghoe

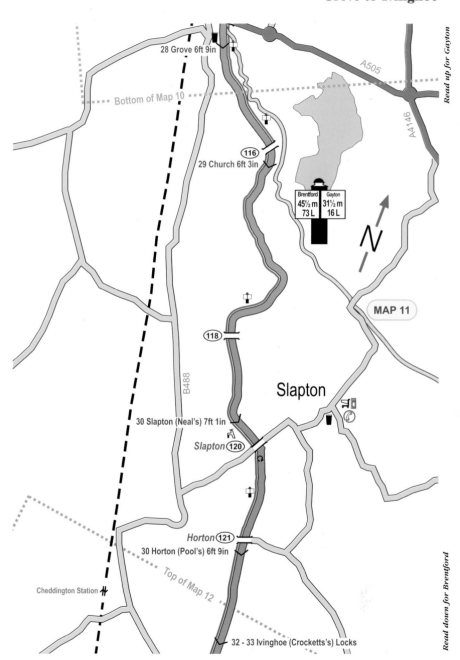

28 Grove 6ft 9in

A505

Read up for Gayton

Bottom of Map 10

A4146

116

29 Church 6ft 3in

Brentford	Gayton
45½ m	31½ m
73 L	16 L

MAP 11

118

B488

Slapton

30 Slapton (Neal's) 7ft 1in

Slapton 120

Horton 121

30 Horton (Pool's) 6ft 9in

Top of Map 12

Cheddington Station

Read down for Brentford

32 - 33 Ivinghoe (Crocketts's) Locks

Seabrook Locks

One with a substantial Grand Junction pumping engine house alongside, these locks lift the canal up to Pitstone Wharf. Bridge 125 is a working swing bridge. Ivinghoe Beacon to the east is almost 760ft high.

Pitstone 🍴 🅒 ⛴️ 🍴🔭

A largely residential settlement which served the huge cement works, which stand before a backdrop of the Chilterns. The *Duke of Wellington* has Fullers, Marstons, Ruddles and Flowers beers and ciders and offers food every lunchtime and evening. It also has a garden. There is a Chinese restaurant by the roundabout as well as a newsagent and general store/off licence. Pitstone Post Mill contains timbers dated 1627 making it the earliest windmill still standing. National Trust 01582 872303) open June–Aug, Sun & Bank Hol Mon 2.30–5.30pm.

Ivinghoe 🍴 🅘 🍴 ⛴️ 🚗 *Early Closing Wed.* The inspiration for Walter Scott's *Ivanhoe,* though only in name. A walk up the road to the village from Ivinghoe Road Bridge (123) will lead past Ford End Water Mill, but one from Bridge 126 will take you close by Pitstone Green Museum. The 13th century church of St Mary the Virgin contains some well preserved carvings, and the *Kings Head* (01296 668388) is comfortably ancient, with oak beams and inglenook fireplaces though its restaurant is pricey and a dress code operates, which may exclude many! However, specialities include Aylesbury Duckling. Ivinghoe Post Office stocks souvenirs – it closes at mid-day on Wednesday and Saturday. At the top of the village is the National Trust's Pitstone Post Mill.

Ford End Water Mill (01582 600391) is the only working water mill to survive intact in Buckinghamshire and is open on occasional summer weekend afternoons.

Pitstone Green Museum in Vicarage Road (01582 605464) covers local rural life and trades as well as having a full-size section of a Lancaster bomber. Opening is very limited, or by appointment, so check in advance.

Cheddington 🍴🍴 🅒 🅘 *Early Closing Thur.* The *Swan* is a charming old pub set back from the road. It serves Tetley and guest beers with food available every lunchtime and evening (except Sunday evenings) in the restaurant and bar. The *Three Horseshoes* is open all day at weekends offering lunches every day except Sunday. The general store is open Sun morning. Beyond Cheddington is Mentmore Towers, completed in 1854 for Baron Rothschild in the Tudor style of Wollaton Hall by architect Joseph Paxton. The grounds are open daily and there are afternoon tours of the house (01296 661881).

Grebe Canal Cruises 🍴 🅛 🅘 ⛴️ 🅗🚗 🅜 🅑 🅒 🛒 (01296 661920). Boat Safety Scheme inspections, repairs & maintenance, fitting out, breakdowns, slipway. Shop sells chandlery, souvenirs, gifts & ice cream. Trip boats: up to 60 passengers. Regular daily & weekend trips, charter and educational. Self-drive day boats

Bridges 126 – Marsworth

The Duke of Wellington close to Bridge 126 serves Fullers, Marstons, Ruddles and Flowers beers, ciders and lagers, and food every lunchtime and evening. West of Bridge 126, Artist Brian Pitman specialises in canal paintings and miniatures.

Past the Dunstable & District Boat Club moorings is Marsworth Bottom Lock, lock 38 and, the former *Ship Inn,* now a private house.

Marsworth 🍴 🅒 🅘 🍴🔭

Known to generations of boatmen as 'Maffers' – a tradition that persists today in some quarters, this is a pleasant and popular port of call, with several good pubs, some interesting walks and the Tring reservoirs to explore. Marsworth locks swing round the village in a graceful curve, mak-

MAP 12
Pitstone to Marsworth

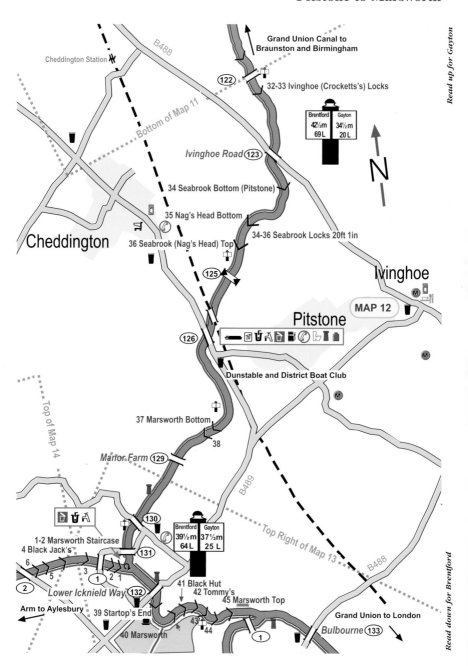

Read up for Gayton

Cheddington Station

B488

Bottom of Map 11

Grand Union Canal to
Braunston and Birmingham

(122) 32-33 Ivinghoe (Crocketts's) Locks

Brentford	Gayton
42½m	34½m
69 L	20 L

Ivinghoe Road (123)

N

34 Seabrook Bottom (Pitstone)

35 Nag's Head Bottom

Cheddington

34-36 Seabrook Locks 20ft 1in

36 Seabrook (Nag's Head) Top

(125)

Ivinghoe

(126)

MAP 12

Pitstone

Dunstable and District Boat Club

Top of Map 14

37 Marsworth Bottom

38

Manor Farm (129)

B489

Top Right of Map 13

B488

1-2 Marsworth Staircase
4 Black Jack's

(130)

Brentford	Gayton
39½m	37½m
64 L	25 L

(131)

6   5   3   2 1
(2)

41 Black Hut
42 Tommy's

45 Marsworth Top

Lower Icknield Way (132)

43 44

Grand Union to London

39 Startop's End

Arm to Aylesbury

40 Marsworth

(1)

Bulbourne (133)

Read down for Brentford

Robin Smitbett

British Waterways' former Maintenance Yard at Bulbourne retains its attractive workshop buildings.

ing this perhaps the most attractive flight on the Grand Union. The *Red Lion* near Bridge 130, selling Vale Brewery and Fullers beers, is the 'boating' pub. It's also in the *Good Beer Guide* and likes to be described as "a proper pub with 90% beer and 10% food"! Meals are available Tue–Sat lunchtimes and evening but only at lunch time on Sunday and Monday. The pub is open all day in summer. There's bar billiards, and families and muddy dogs are welcome. The *White Lion* by Bridge 132 serves Speckled Hen and regularly changing guest ales and has an extensive bar meals menu with restauarant meals in addition during the evening. It is open all day every day. The *Angler's Retreat* is a cosy 'local' doing bar meals all day every day and Fullers and Batemans beers. By Startop's End Lock is the Blue Bells (01442 891708) providing homemade cakes, herbal teas, fresh coffee, ices and other delicacies with a garden in which to enjoy

them. It is open from 10am–5pm (or dusk) Mon–Sat and 9am–5pm on Sundays.

British Waterways, Marsworth Junction

As this guide was completed British Waterways announced closure of this office although the facilities remained available. See page 15 for details of BW's offices which are no longer at the water's edge. Much of the Grand Union Canal and the river Lee are lined with concrete piles made in the adjacent buildings in the 1950s and '60s.

The Aylesbury Arm drops away from Marsworth Junction via a two-rise staircase. (See page 52.)

From Marsworth north to Stoke Bruerne the main line locks were duplicated during the 1830s to speed traffic. Signs of these locks, long since infilled, and some double-arched bridges remain.

MAP 13
Marsworth

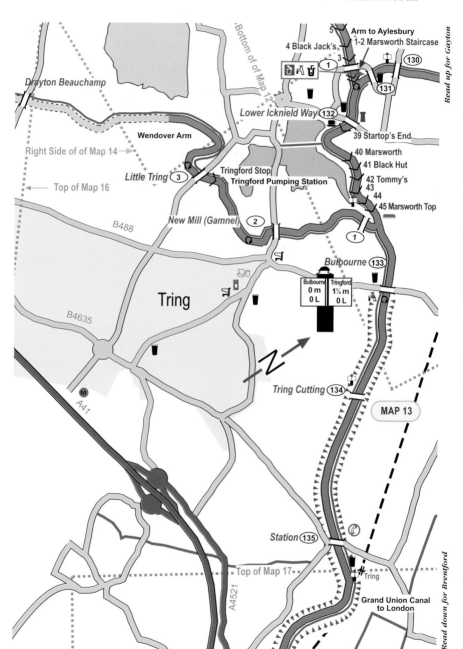

Read up for Gayton

5
Arm to Aylesbury
4 Black Jack's
1-2 Marsworth Staircase
3
130
1
131

Bottom of Map 12

Drayton Beauchamp

Lower Icknield Way 132

Wendover Arm

39 Startop's End

Right Side of of Map 14 →

40 Marsworth
41 Black Hut

Little Tring 3

Tringford Stop
Tringford Pumping Station

42 Tommy's
43
44
45 Marsworth Top

Top of Map 16 ←

New Mill (Gamnel) 2

1

B488

Bulbourne 133

Bulbourne	Tringford
0 m	1¼ m
0 L	0 L

Tring

B4635

Tring Cutting 134

MAP 13

A41

Station 135

Top of Map 17

Tring

A4521

Grand Union Canal
to London

Read down for Brentford

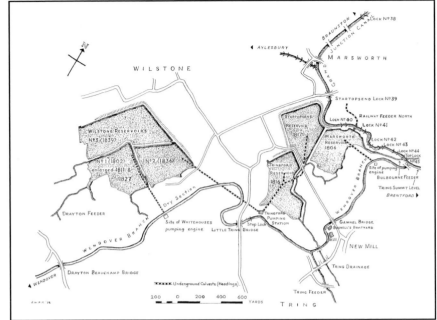

Edward Paget-Tomlinson

The complex of reservoirs which was gradually built up to ensure a water supply to the Tring Summit. The main line of the Grand Junction part of the Grand Union Canal presented severe water supply problems, passing as it does over two summits between Braunston and the Thames. In a world of silent electric pumps and remote computerized control, few modern boaters appreciate the difficulties that canal engineers of the past faced in keeping trade afloat.

Marsworth Locks and Bulbourne

Marsworth Locks are pleasant to work. At the top is the drydock and the entrance to the Wendover Arm (see pages 57–59).

This is the famous Tring Summit, subject of the controversial Improvement Scheme of the 1970s which saw a 21 mile length earmarked for sometimes actual, more usually cosmetic, maintenance which delighted visiting dignitaries but raised serious questions about the economical merit of the scheme. Eventually only 8 miles were treated, from Marsworth to Dudswell, and for a few years the Tring Summit became the star of the waterways, achieving the admirable objective of showing how all Britain's canals could look given the money. Now some years later,

the paint, like the memory has faded and there is little to show for the thousands it cost. That is, with the exception of the commendable refurbishment done to the magnificent Bulbourne Depot, where the architectural mix of practical simplicity and style is a delight to the eye. Built largely in 1848 when lock-gate production was transferred from Paddington,

Tring Reservoirs

Built to supply the canal with water these reservoirs became an official wildlife reserve in 1955, with the HQ of the British Trust for Ornithology nearby. Rare animals and plants abound, from migrant and breeding birds and the black poplar to the edible dormouse or *Glis glis*. The Nature Conservancy Council has published a highly informative booklet about the reservoirs.

Bulbourne 🍺 ©

This hamlet owes its existence to the canal and its workshops, an origin reflected in the name of the pub, the *Grand Junction Arms*. This is a busy but friendly pub offering Adnams, Flowers, Courage and guest beers and food every weekday lunchtime and evening as well as all day on Saturdays and Sundays. Specialties include curries and regional buffets. There is often Jazz or Blues music on Sundays (01442 890677). Summer barbecues, canalside garden, moorings.

Tring *All services,* variously 1½–2 miles. Paco Chinese Takeaway (01442 852069) will deliver. Don't miss the Walter Rothschild Zoological Museum in Akeman Street (020 7942 6171, www.nhm.ac.uk/museum/tring).

Bulbourne workshops where fittings and lock gates for the Grand Union were made.

Founded on a bequest by the late Lord Walter Rothschild of a large collection of rare crustacea and insects, this museum is now affiliated to the Natural History Museum. The *King's Arms* is a free house. The pub is *Good Beer Guide* listed, and serves a range of real ales. Bar food is available every lunchtime and evening from 7pm. Children are welcome. Also in the *Good Beer Guide* is the *Robin Hood* in Brook Street, which offers Fullers beer and a menu specialising in seafood dishes. Moor by Tring Station or at Bulbourne for the 1½ mile walk, or take a bus.

Bridges 133–136

Whatever the time of year, passage through Tring Cutting is memorable, with a spectacular array of trees. Part of the 'Improvement Scheme' involved cutting back the vegetation but, thankfully, the effect has enhanced, not detracted. The towpath is still good. Bridge 134 has a standard arch but very tall parapet and no access. At Station Bridge it is possible to moor and walk up to Tring Station.

Grand Union Main Line south to Brentford continues on page 60, Map 17.

For **Aylesbury Arm** see pages 52–56, Maps 14 & 15.

For **Wendover Arm** see pages 57–59, Map 16.

Historical Introduction

Though authorisation for a branch of the Grand Junction (GJ) to serve Aylesbury was included in the act of 1793 nothing was actually done for another 20 years. This was largely because the GJ was not particularly keen, foreseeing the effect such a canal would have upon its water supplies. Despite this, the GJ was persuaded otherwise by the enthusiasm of the people of Aylesbury, supported by the Marquis of Buckingham, and the announcement of plans for a link between Marsworth and the Thames at Abingdon. The new canal was to be known as the Western Junction and would form a link with the Wiltshire & Berkshire Canal (W&B), so cutting a vast London loop off the trip to the West Country. It was to be a joint scheme, the GJ to build the line to Aylesbury and private enterprise, aided by the W&B, to complete the course. Unfortunately, so strong was the opposition from affected waterways and landowners that hopes for the route west of Aylesbury failed, but the GJ kept its side of the deal and completed the 6¼ mile arm, which falls 94ft 8in through 16 locks to Aylesbury, in 1815.

The branch was built narrow to minimise the demand for water but, nevertheless, the loss proved substantial and Wilstone Reservoir was enlarged twice in an attempt to alleviate the problem. Traffic was brisk both ways, with coal, timber and building materials arriving in Aylesbury while agricultural produce, hay and livestock went out. Industry too was attracted to the canalside town and the Aylesbury Condensed Milk Company was established in 1870, now Nestlé. Railway competition was severe but the canal survived as a commercial route through to the 1950s when the firm of Harvey-Taylor ceased commercial trading. Traffic thereafter was sporadic. Deterioration was rapid after this, in spite of the establishment of a hire firm and the holding of an IWA rally in 1961. The wharfside buildings in Aylesbury were demolished and the silt grew thick but, in 1973, the Aylesbury Canal Society (ACS) was formed. Restoration work began and today the future of the arm is assured. However, British Waterways and the local authorities continue to produce development proposals that may eventually destroy what remains of the original surroundings of the basin with 'Disney-fication' and twee houses – even a hotel. The ACS publish an excellent and inexpensive booklet to the picturesque canal, which provides an entertaining companion to the journey.

A few of the locks will require a BW yale key to release the security locks.

Marsworth 🍴🍺 Ⓒ 🚻 ♒

See page 46–50 for full details.

Bridges 1–3

Within yards of the junction the Aylesbury Arm establishes a character most emphatically 'all its own'. The narrow locks, 16 of them, begin with a two-chambered staircase that requires just a little thought. Going down, fill the upper chamber and enter the lock. Close the top paddles. Check that the lower chamber is empty and its bottom paddles closed before you discharge the upper chamber into it using the middle paddle. Move through to the lower lock and work down as normal. Rising up, again you will need a full top chamber to lift the boat out of the lower one. No more than one set of paddles should be raised at any one time. (See also page 10.)

Wilstone 🍴🍺 Ⓒ 🚻 ♒

A short walk leads to this village where you'll find the *Half Moon*, an ABC pub. The PO/Stores opens daily ex Sat and Sun afternoons. Swimming is permitted in Wilstone Reservoir, beyond the village, in spite of its being a nature reserve. As well as supplying the Aylesbury Arm, its waters are also drawn up onto Tring Summit by the Tringford pumps.

MAP 14

Aylesbury Arm – Marsworth to Redhouse

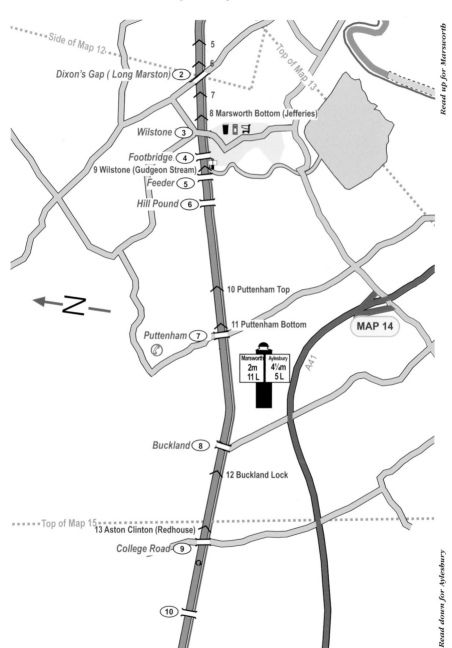

Side of Map 12

Top of Map 13

Read up for Marsworth

5

6

Dixon's Gap (Long Marston) ②

7

8 Marsworth Bottom (Jefferies)

Wilstone ③

Footbridge ④

9 Wilstone (Gudgeon Stream)

Feeder ⑤

Hill Pound ⑥

←N–

10 Puttenham Top

11 Puttenham Bottom

Puttenham ⑦

MAP 14

A41

Marsworth	Aylesbury
2m	4¼m
11 L	5 L

Buckland ⑧

12 Buckland Lock

Top of Map 15

13 Aston Clinton (Redhouse)

College Road ⑨

Read down for Aylesbury

⑩

Bridges 4–11

Passing the reservoir feeder by Bridge 5 the canal passes through a short cutting, the only one on the canal, to reappear amid yet more open farmland. The tiny agricultural hamlet of Puttenham (½mile north, telephone box) has a remarkably original medieval church. Its most famous incumbent was the turncoat Christopher Urswick who, as Recorder of London under Richard III, was able to serve the exiled Henry Tudor with valuable information, warn him of an attempted kidnap and later marry him to Edward IV's daughter, Elizabeth. The canal, continuing its fall to Aylesbury, passes Buckland and Aston Clinton, both some short walk to the south. The Aston Clinton Boat Club (formerly Aylesbury Pleasure Boat Centre) has its moorings by Bridge 9. The Red House was once a pub.

Though the arm is very straight and undeniably man-made, any risk of monotony is amply overcome by the delightfully rustic scenery through which it passes. Wildlife, both floral and fauna, abounds along its margins and the lush farmland of the Aylesbury Vale spreads away to the horizon.

Buckland ⌐◖ ▯

A straggling hamlet drawn out along the narrow road ¾mile from the canal. There's a small shop but, by the time you find the *Rothschild Arms* (ABC and substantial bar meals, ex Sun) you're in Aston Clinton.

Aston Clinton ⌐▮ ◖ ▯ ♈ ⌐⊪

🚗 The village is now separated from the Aylesbury Arm by the A41 Aston Clinton Bypass and is about 1½ miles from Bridge 8. (See page 58)

Broughton
A 2-mile pound, the longest on the canal, ends at Broughton Lock, where one can visit the *Prince of Wales* at Broughton Crossing. This friendly Pubmaster house serves snacks and has a garden. It stands beyond the disused level crossing of the Aylesbury–

Cheddington line. Broughton proper lies to the south and consists of only a few houses and Oak Farm Rare Breeds Park, which is open from Easter to October. Children must take an adult along but no dogs and will be able to see a variety of farm animals (01296 415709, www.pebblesculpt.co.uk/oakfarm).

Bridges 15–18

No access at Oakfield Bridge. The final approach to Aylesbury is not the anti-climax it might be and the canal is bounded by parkland and trees which extend to the factories, where willows, ash and alder disguise the harshness of brick and corrugated iron. The Bear Brook, running down from Aston Clinton, passes under the canal above Lock 15.

Aylesbury Basin ▮ ▮ ⌂ ♈ ▣

The basin is more exposed now that many original buildings have gone, and brightly painted boats fill most available spaces. Visitors are assured of a warm welcome from members of the Aylesbury Canal Society, who have been looking after the basin since 1973. Several members live afloat and they have a clubhouse here, so there's always someone around – watch for the 'Welcome Boat' sign. The *Ship Inn* (Marstons and Greene King, bar meals at lunch time and pool table) stands at the entrance to the basin.

Aylesbury *All services, Early Closing Thurs, Market Day Wed & Sat. Tourist Information Centre: 8 Bourbon Street, Aylesbury, Buckinghamshire HP20 2RR (Tel/Fax 01296 330559, www.aylesburyvale.net).* A&E at Stoke Mandeville Hospital but always dial 999 first in an emergency. Aylesbury also has a 'Town Centre Manager' if you need further information (01296 396370).

A market town, bustling with life and interest, much of it only a short walk from the canal. Though Aylesbury was strongly Parliamentarian during the Civil War – raising a statue to local hero John Hampden in the cobbled Market Square –

MAP 15
Aylesbury Arm – Aylesbury

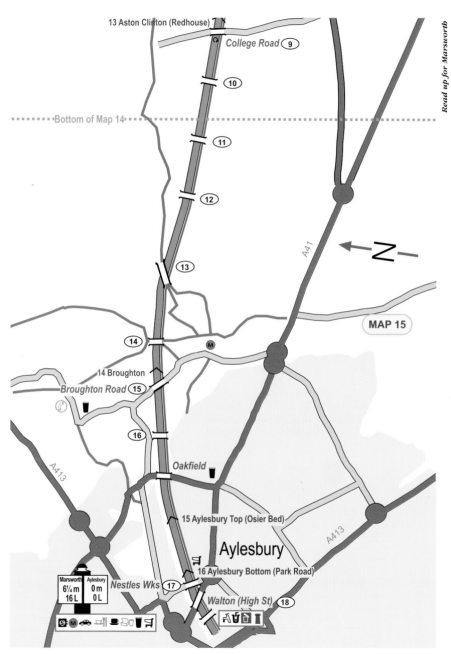

13 Aston Clinton (Redhouse)

College Road ⑨

⑩

Bottom of Map 14

⑪

⑫

⑬

A41

MAP 15

⑭

Ⓜ

14 Broughton

Broughton Road ⑮

⑯

A413

Oakfield

15 Aylesbury Top (Osier Bed)

A413

Aylesbury

16 Aylesbury Bottom (Park Road)

Nestles Wks ⑰

Walton (High St) ⑱

Marsworth	Aylesbury
6¼ m	0 m
16 L	0 L

Read up for Marsworth

Aylesbury Arm

Robin Smithett

Aylesbury Basin is home to a number of residential boats and the moorings of the Canal Society who make visitors most welcome but it is also threatened with redevelopment of much of the land in the background of this view.

the town shows evidence of having attracted royalty. During the past 1500 years few monarchs seem to have missed the town and many buildings boast royal patronage, especially inns. Notable is the *King's Head*, built in 1386, which contains some magnificent leaded windows and 'Cromwell's Chair'. Equality is, perhaps, provided by the *Good Beer Guide* listed *Queen's Head* which is in Temple Square and has Adnams, Courage and Greene King beers as well as lunch. Worth exploring are the many back alleys and passageways which riddle old Aylesbury down one of which is the *Dark Lantern*, a 16th century inn. The County Museum in Church Street (01296 331441, www.buckscc.gov.uk/museum) has displays of archeology, natural history, art and local history as well as a Roald Dahl Childrens'

Gallery and organizes talks and special events. It is open from 10am–5pm Mon–Sat as well as 2–5pm on Sundays.

Eating & Drinking. Aylesbury has a wide variety of pubs and restaurants. Pubs other than those already mentioned Include the *Bricklayers Arms* (south of Bridge 19).

There's a large new swimming pool and fitness centre in Park Street. The new Civic Centre hosts concerts, exhibitions and shows, and is fully licensed (01296 486009) and the six-screen Odeon Cinema is adjacent.

For Grand Union Main Line north to Gayton go to page 51 and Map 13.
For Grand Union Main Line south to Brentford go to page 60, Map 17.

Introduction and History

Originally this 6¾ mile arm was seen only as a feeder, but under the Grand Union Canal's 1794 Act authority was given for navigation. Drawing on wells in Wendover and gathering water from sources in Weston Turville and Halton, the canal was the only original feeder for the summit but proved most inadequate. In 1802 a reservoir was built at Wilstone, followed by those at Marsworth in 1806, Tringford in 1816 and Startop's End in 1817. Wilstone was enlarged twice, in 1836 and 1839, giving an indication of the traffic in those busy years. Of the various reservoirs, Wilstone 1 & 2 and Tringford connected with the Wendover Arm via the Tringford pumps, while overflow supplied Marsworth and Startop's End. Though carrying a limited amount of traffic, the arm was never a commercial goldmine, a feature made worse by maintenance problems posed by the porous ground base. Extensive puddling and even lining with asphalt failed to overcome the water loss, which at times exceeded the volume fed into the arm. Eventually a stop lock was built at Tringford, which only highlighted the weakness, as the water beyond tended to disappear in summer, forcing abandonment of the arm west of the lock in 1904.

Marsworth to Little Tring

The first 1½ miles (see Map 13, page 49) remained to be well used, both as a feeder from the pumping station and also by the famous Bushell Brothers boatbuilding yard at New Mill. Such famous boats as the wide-beam *Progress* and *Golden Spray* came from this yard. When the yard closed all traffic on the arm went with it. Also at New Mill, Heygates flour mill adds industrial interest to an otherwise rural route.

Overgrown with weed and heavily silted, few ventured up the arm until the Wendover Arm Trust took it under their wing and embarked on restoration. In 1982 British Waterways dredged the first 1½ miles, restored the stop lock and reinstated the towpath. Boats of up to about 50ft may wind just beyond New Mill. Smaller craft (and those skilled at reversing longer ones) have been able to navigate to the stop lock at Tringford Pumping Station since 1982. This is about to change. Little Tring Bridge has now been reconstructed and work is almost complete on a winding hole for full length craft a short distance beyond.

Grand Union Canal Society and Manpower Services Commission work groups have re-opened the towpath and it is now feasible to walk through to Wendover. The Wendover Arm Trust publishes a booklet that will be useful to explorers, see Bibliography (page 14). To encourage the use of the arm, the Trust offers a certificate and brass plaque to those providing proof of navigation to Tringford. (Send to the Secretary; see page 16.)

With modern techniques to overcome the leakage problems there are now plans for complete restoration.

New Mill ⌷▌ⓒ▯

Though Tring is several miles from the canal there are shops closer to the main line or Wendover Arm at Tring Wharf, near New Mill.

Little Tring to Buckland

The underground culvert from Wilstone reservoirs to Tringford pumping station passes beneath the arm beyond the new winding hole. Along the next section, at a point known as Whitehouses (despite the demolition of the eponymous cottages as long ago as the early 1950s), is the site of the inlet to the culvert from which canal water was run into the reservoirs in times of plenty. A pumping engine supplied well water to the canal here until superceded by the Tringford pump in 1835. This section of the arm was the most troublesome and leak-ridden until it was finally abandoned in 1904. The first total closure of the arm between Whitehouses and Marsworth in an attempt to cure leaks had been as long ago as 1804!

Rothschild Bridge at Halton on the Wendover Arm has been restored, but, as yet, only for the enjoyment of walkers although restoration of the navigation is progressing towards the site.

Beyond Buckland Wharf the canal has been more likely to hold water. Here the waterway has been moved onto a new line as part of the construction of the A41 Aston Clinton By-pass. As part of the works the sump where the canal's water disappears into the pipe which carries it to Tringford is being moved east of Drayton Beauchamp Bridge.

Aston Clinton 🍴🍺 🅒 📱♿ ⚓

Aston Clinton owes much to the Rothschilds, who settled here in 1851 and, though their house has been demolished, evidence of their presence remains. The village has been greatly improved by the removal of through traffic to the A41 bypass. *The Oak* echoes this trend towards greater civilization by having no piped music or machines but it does offer Fullers beers and bar meals every lunch time and on all but Sunday evenings. There are five pubs, the most famous of which is the *Bell*, an historic coaching inn with a highly regarded restaurant housed in a large conservatory.

Green Park to Weston Turville

The canal continues through attractive parkland now and a narrowed section of this once wide waterway to the extensive RAF camp at Halton. Halton is centred south of the canal and beyond are tranquil walks in the National Trust's Wendover Woods. The ornate, iron, Rothschild Bridge, built by banker Alfred de Rothschild in 1880 is now restored and Grade II listed. The road bridge at Halton will need to be raised or replaced by a moveable structure to allow navigation to the terminus. On the way Weston Turville reservoir is passed; it was built by the Grand Junction company to hold compensation water for the millers of Aylesbury – to keep their water wheels turning after their original supply had been diverted into the canal.

Wendover *All Services. Market Day Thur. Tourist Info: The Clock Tower, High Street, Wendover, Buckinghamshire HP22 6DU (01296 696759, Fax: 01296 622460).* The canal creeps peacefully under a footbridge built on the line of the railway to Halton Camp, and past silted wides and the former wharf to end at a gauging sluice where the water from Wendover Springs enters the navigation. Records of the water flow here exist back to 1841 – the earliest continuous flow measurements in England.

Wendover can provide all your needs including trains or buses to carry walkers back to their starting points. Also walker-friendly is the *Red Lion* (01296 622266) on the High Street which has B&B accomodation and serves Youngs and Brakspear's as well as guest beers and home cooked food is available seven days a week (all day Sundays). There is also a bank, Indian takeaway, fish & chips, and convenience store with cash machine, as well as further pubs. The Tourist Office can provide a series of excellent guided walk leaflets, some routes include the canal towpath.

For Grand Union Main Line north to Gayton go to page 51 and Map 13.
For Grand Union Main Line south to Brentford go to page 60, Map 17.

MAP 16
Wendover Arm – Buckland to Wendover

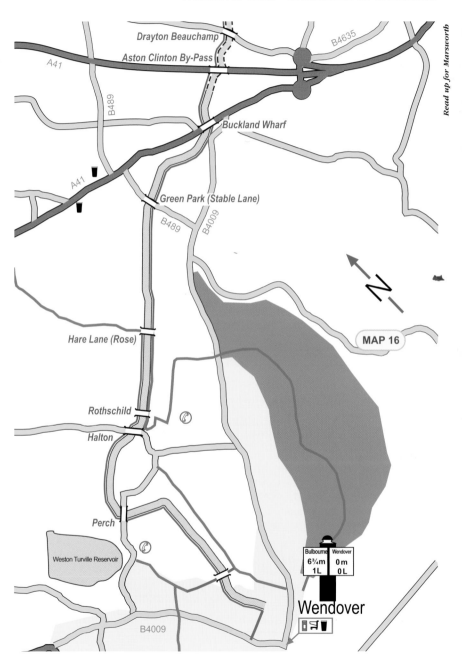

Read up for Marsworth

Drayton Beauchamp
B4635
Aston Clinton By-Pass
A41
B489
Buckland Wharf
A41
Green Park (Stable Lane)
B489
B4009

N

MAP 16

Hare Lane (Rose)

Rothschild
Halton

Perch

Weston Turville Reservoir

Bulbourne	Wendover
6¾m	0 m
1L	0 L

Wendover

B4009

Main Line – Aldbury to Northchurch

For **Grand Union Main Line** north to Gayton go to page 51 and Map 13.

Aldbury ▮ ⓒ 🚗 🎣▯ ☕

Cash machine at PO/general store. It's a good mile's walk to the village, arranged round the green with pond, shady tree and stocks. There is an occasional bus! The *Greyhound* makes the walk worthwhile offering Badger beers and lagers with food every lunchtime and on all but Sunday evenings; book for the 'Special walker's Sunday breakfast' (01442 851228). Nearby is the *Valiant Trooper* (01442 851203) offering London Pride and guest real ales all day and food (not Sun eve or Mon).

Struggling bravely to be seen above the trees is the copper-green urn of the 200ft Bridgewater Monument, a further half a mile beyond the village. Erected in 1832 to honour Francis, Third Duke of Bridgewater 'Father of Inland Navigation' it contains 172 steps and offers fine views of the Aylesbury Vale. It stands in Ashridge Park, now managed by the National Trust but once part of the Bridgewater estates. The Park is open all year but the Visitor Centre, which has attractive displays of the area, some interactive, only in the afternoons Apr–Oct with access to the monument itself at weekends or on Bank Holidays. The shop has a good range of books and souvenirs.

Tring Buffer Depot is on the offside of the canal north of Bridge 136. Amongst the modern industrial buildings is one of a number of identical warehouses that were built around the canal system during the Second World War to hold rationed food supplies which were dispersed by water transport to reduce the chance of destruction by enemy action.

Cowroast ▮ 🔥 ♨ 🎣▮ 🚗 ⓒ

Nothing to do with cooking, we are told, but derived from cow rest, since this was a popular overnight stop for cattle drovers heading for the London markets. The *Cowroast Inn* (Spitfire, Abbott, Youngs and Fullers) has everything to do with cooking, with a varied menu available. Meals are served every lunchtime and on weekday evenings. The pub is open all day every day. The nearby garage can provide milk, bread, tea, and coffee etc, as well as petrol. Cowroast Lock marks the end of the canal's rise from the Thames, some 393ft below. For southbound boaters it's now downhill all the way to the river.

Cowroast Marina 🚽 🏧 🗄️🗄️🛢️ (01442 823222, www.cowroastmarinas. co.uk). Repairs and maintenance, breakdowns (not 24hr), boatfitting, steel fabrication, drydock, wetdock, slipway to 70ft, hardstanding, moorings, Boat Safety Scheme inspections, brokerage and insurance. Shop sells extensive chandlery, souvenirs, maps, guides, etc.

Dudswell Locks ⓒ

This pair of locks marks the southern limit of the Tring Improvement Scheme, originally envisaged as a 21 mile showpiece from Northchurch to Soulbury, but eventually consisting of only an 8 mile section between here and Marsworth. There's a phone box in Dudswell!

Northchurch ▮ ⓒ 🎣▮

Near the canal is 'new' Northchurch, reminiscent of Milton Keynes in some respects, but up by the main road is the ancient flint church, dating from Saxon times and one of the world's oldest. It contains a handsome 15th century Flemish chest and several colourful stained glass windows. The *George & Dragon*, near Bridge 139, serves bar food Mon–Sat and Benskins. The *Old Grey Mare* offers full bar meals every day. Up from Bridge 140 is the *Crooked Billet* and some small shops leading to the *Rose & Crown* and a sports & leisure centre.

MAP 17
Aldbury to Berkhamsted

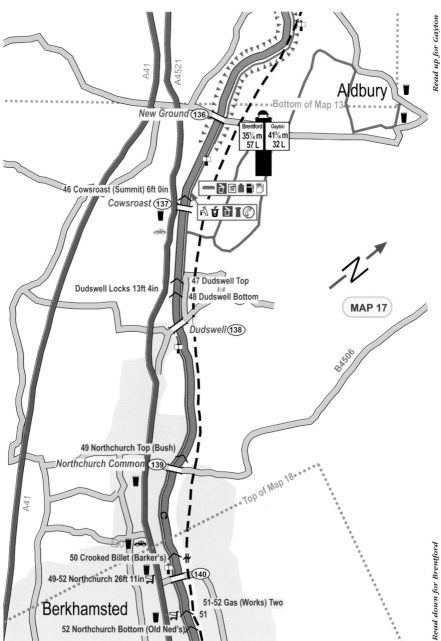

Read up for Gayton

Aldbury

Bottom of Map 13

New Ground 136

Brentford	Gayton
35¼ m	41¾ m
57 L	32 L

46 Cowsroast (Summit) 6ft 0in

Cowsroast 137

47 Dudswell Top

Dudswell Locks 13ft 4in

48 Dudswell Bottom

Dudswell 138

MAP 17

B4506

49 Northchurch Top (Bush)

Northchurch Common 139

Top of Map 18

50 Crooked Billet (Barker's)

49-52 Northchurch 26ft 11in 140

51-52 Gas (Works) Two

Berkhamsted

51

52 Northchurch Bottom (Old Ned's)

A41

A4521

Read down for Brentford

Berkhamsted *All services, Early Closing Wed, Market Day Sat. Laundrette.*

Strung out along the A4251, Berkhamsted bustles with shoppers too busy to notice old churches, inns, public buildings and the remains of a Norman castle. This was a gift from William the Conqueror to his half-brother Robert. Thomas à Becket spent time here as Chancellor and in 1216 it was besieged by the barons, eager to teach King John a lesson. In 1336 it passed to the Black Prince and the Duchy of Cornwall, where it has remained whenever there's been a Prince of Wales to hold the title. The castle was rebuilt in the 12th century but again fell into disrepair during the 16th century and a new residence, Berkhamsted Palace was built. In 1930 the castle was placed into the Nation's care and is now maintained by English Heritage. The massive earthworks and twin moats are very impressive. Of other buildings: St Peter's is a large flint-built church containing numerous brasses and monuments. Incent House, near the church, is a carefully restored half-timbered building of the 16th century. Several pubs are of architectural interest, including the plastered and gabled *Bell Inn* and the bay-fronted *King's Arms Hotel* which has a restaurant for which booking is advised (01442 866595) and which offers a wide menu with tea and coffee available all day. There is also accomodation.

Berkhamsted has numerous Indian restaurants and takeaways, a Chinese takeaway, and coffee and wine bars. There are both Tesco and Waitrose supermarkets and an organic butcher is to be found up Gravel Path opposite the *Boat* pub.

There are several canalside pubs in Berkhamsted. The *Crystal Palace* (Bridge 141) is resplendent with colourful hanging baskets in summer and has good moorings. It is open all day and the beer is Moorland, Greene King and Adnams; food is available every lunch and evening. The *Boat Inn* is a Fullers house serving a wide selection of bar food all day and having a big screen TV. Overlooking Lock 54 the *Rising Sun* has a pleasant lockside terrace. Below Lock 55 is the *Bull*, a famous boating pub with moorings, bar meals and Benskins. Near Bridge 143 is the *Old Mill House* (Courage with snacks and full restaurant meals including vegetarian choices) while at the other end of the town we found Indian and Chinese restaurants and the *Lamb Inn*. On the main street are the *Penny Farthing* and associated *Café Rouge Restaurant & Hotel* and several takeaways. Woods Garden Centre near Bridge 140B sells Gaz, local cards and souvenirs. The *Goat* is at the top of Ravens Lane serving Landlord and Pedigree, cider and Mexican food on Tue–Sat eves as well as lunchtime snacks and sandwiches and Sunday lunches (it boasts a "safe" garden).

British Waterways regard Berkhamsted as the northern limit of the Grand Union as a barge canal and broad-beamed craft may proceed further only with special care and need prior booking to pass through the tunnels at Blisworth and Braunston. The town itself clearly appreciates its canal and the houses, parks and light industry tend to look towards rather than away from the waterway. At the site of the wharf of timber importers J. Alsford Ltd by Bridge 141, stands the famous totem pole. It was carved by a Kwakiutl Indian from Vancouver and erected in 1967.

Bourne End and Winkwell

Only a smattering of buildings yet a convivial spot. There are three pubs a hotel and some enjoyable walks to be had. The river Bulbourne passes beneath the bar of the *Hemel Hempstead Moat House*, which occupies the site of an old flour mill by Lock 59. Over the road are two excellent pubs: the *White Horse* (01442 863888) is a large pub serving restaurant meals (booking advised) and an extensive menu of bar food all day; while next door the *Anchor* (open all day) offers sandwiches to go with its Greene

MAP 18
Berkhamsted to Winkwell

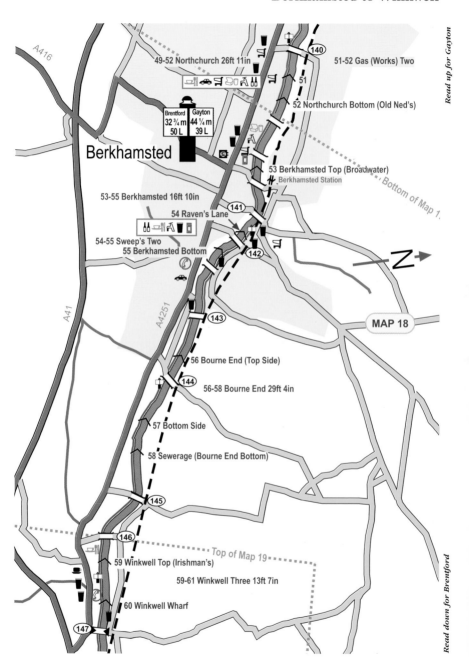

49-52 Northchurch 26ft 11in

51-52 Gas (Works) Two

140

51

52 Northchurch Bottom (Old Ned's)

Brentford	Gayton
32 ¾ m	44 ¼ m
50 L	39 L

Berkhamsted

53 Berkhamsted Top (Broadwater)

Berkhamsted Station

Bottom of Map 1.

53-55 Berkhamsted 16ft 10in

54 Raven's Lane

141

54-55 Sweep's Two

55 Berkhamsted Bottom

142

Z

MAP 18

143

56 Bourne End (Top Side)

144

56-58 Bourne End 29ft 4in

57 Bottom Side

58 Sewerage (Bourne End Bottom)

145

146

Top of Map 19

59 Winkwell Top (Irishman's)

59-61 Winkwell Three 13ft 7in

60 Winkwell Wharf

147

King and Flowers ales. The *Three Horseshoes* is beside Winkwell Swing Bridge. It offers home cooked meals every lunchtime and evening (except Sun eve) with regularly changing menus and is open all day every day. The bridge, which is electrically operated, requires a BW sanitary station key. Check for road traffic and follow the instructions carefully.

Middlesex & Hertfordshire Boat Services ⚓ 🛥 🏧 🔧 🍴 🏪 🛒 Winkwell Dock. (01442 872985, Fax 01442 863394, www.mhboatservices.co.uk). Moorings, including residential, showers, chandlery, engine repairs and breakdown service, solid fuel, storage, boat sales, slipway, cranage, boatbuilding, fitting out, dustless sandblasting and painting, brokerage, laundrette. Closed Mon.

Bridges 145–148

Dropping through a series of evenly-spaced locks the canal continues its fall to the Thames – or nears the end of its climb, depending upon your direction. It is not easy work but the scenery is rewarding and only the railway intrudes. Trains are frequent as are stations en-route. Various rivers accompany the canal: the Bulbourne here and the Gade through to Batchworth feeding water into the canal, flooding the watercress beds and encouraging wildlife; Little Grebe seem locally common.

Boxmoor 🍺 ☕ 🏪

The *Swan* (London Pride and Speckled Hen), beyond the railway from Bridge 148, is open all day every day and has bar meals every lunch and evening except Sunday, and live music at weekends. A Roman villa was discovered in grounds behind the pub. Next door is the *Boxmoor Lodge Hotel*, whose restaurant is open at lunchtimes Tue–Fri and evenings Mon–Sat (01442 203770, www.boxmoorlodge.co.uk). The former Hemel Hempstead Station Cafe is a Chinese takeaway. Many rare breeds of cattle and sheep, which belong to the Boxmoor Trust, can be seen grazing the meadows alongside the canal. The *Fishery Inn* by Bridge 149 occupies an enviable location. It's an Ember Inn serving food all day and has garden moorings. Boxmoor was the destination of the last bastion of commercial traffic. L. Rose & Co, lime juice manufacturers, received the raw, concentrated pulp by boat until 1980, when deliveries to the wharf below Bridge 151, now occupied by a DIY superstore, finally ceased. Set back from Two Waters Bridge is a Balti House. Other hostelries including the *Three Blackbirds*, the *Steam Coach* and the *Heath Park* overlook parkland to the north.

Hemel Hempstead *All services, Early Closing Wed, Market Day Thur, Fri & Sat.* Tourist Info: Marlowes, Hemel Hempstead, Hertfordshire HP1 1DT (01442 234222, Fax 01442 230427, www.dacorum.gov.uk). Half a mile north of Bridge 151, Hemel Hempstead is not just home to Kodak's laboratories, but an excellent shopping centre too. Among the new can be found the very old. Visit the half-timbered *King's Arms*, hidden away up a side alley. St Mary's church is largely Norman but boasts an unusual 14th century leaded 200ft spire. Walk north, past Gadebridge Park and the *Marchmont Arms* to reach quaintly named Piccott's End, where some remarkable 14th century wall paintings were discovered in 1953.

Apsley *Most services.* In the Domesday Book the river Gade was noted for its mills and 900 years later they are still here, now larger and milling paper, not flour. John Dickinson's mills, which dominated the canal with their coal stocks (delivered from the Midlands by a stream of working boats) and towering buildings, not to mention a, one-time, service of non-stop fly-boats working to and from the City Road Basin in London (see page 106) have vanished. In their place are numerous retail outlets, Sainsbury's, etc. In Apsley are the *White Lion, Bell,* the

MAP 19
Winkwell to Apsley

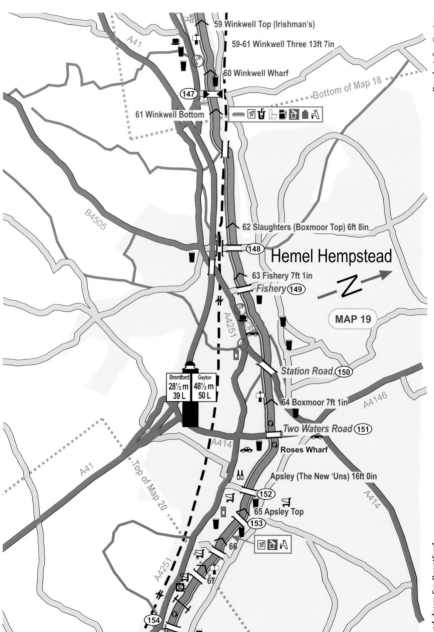

59 Winkwell Top (Irishman's)

59-61 Winkwell Three 13ft 7in

60 Winkwell Wharf

Read up for Gayton

Bottom of Map 18

147

61 Winkwell Bottom

B4505

62 Slaughters (Boxmoor Top) 6ft 8in

148

Hemel Hempstead

63 Fishery 7ft 1in

Fishery 149

MAP 19

A4251

Brentford 28½ m 39 L Gayton 48½ m 50 L

Station Road 150

64 Boxmoor 7ft 1in

A4146

Two Waters Road 151

A414

Roses Wharf

Top of Map 20

A41

Apsley (The New 'Uns) 16ft 0in

152

65 Apsley Top

153

A414

66

A4251

67

154

Read down for Brentford

Spotted Bull and the *Fountain* – access is west of the footbridge below Lock 66.

Swelled by the waters of the Gade which cross by Bridge 151, the canal has a noticeable flow. Bridge 154 has a second, small arch to cope, and the by-weirs roar loudly in winter. The towpath is good and the area is neat, tidy and well presented. Banks of conifers, willow and copper beech hide much of the industry and even the kingfishers approve. Until 1819 the canal course was further to the north, falling through four locks to Kings Langley. This arrangement so disrupted water supplies that Dickinsons insisted it be altered to follow its present course, via five, less thirsty locks. These became known as the 'New 'uns' and Kings Langley Lock was renumbered 69A.

BW Apsley Yard 🏕 ⛴ 🅿 Above Lock 66.

Nash Mills 🍴 🚗 Here the Dickinson Paper Mills survive. Also noteworthy is *Ye Olde Red Lion*. The pub is very popular and serves traditional pub food every lunch & eve – with a non-smoking area at lunchtimes. Booking advised for Sun lunch (01923 262538). North of the canal is the *Three Tuns*, a Benskins house, serving home cooked food and boasting a bouncy castle in the garden as well as music. Reach Out Projects boats are based below the lock. They operate several boats to provide holidays for the handicapped and less fortunate (01707 335968, www.reachoutprojects.org.uk) with skippers and a self steer boat available for hire to youth groups. All are available for day, short break or weekly trips.

Bridges 155–157

For a time we follow the course of the river Gade, a move prompted by the re-alignment of 1819. The channel is wide and deep, bordered by fields and market gardens. Wildfowl drawn to the water include Great Crested Grebes, Canadian Geese, various ducks, swans, coots, and moorhens. The scenery is largely agricultural, though the A41 is never far away.

The working boatmen's names for some Grand Union Canal locks live on, even if the gates are not what you might have expected.

Kings Langley *Most services, Early Closing Wed* . A personable town set back from the canal with excellent facilities, including traditional shops; butchers, Post Office, greengrocers, bakers, paharmacy and several tempting pubs. Toovey's Mill has now gone but memory of their boats remains: *Golden Spray*, built in 1922 was so lavishly decorated that the lettering was even gold leaf! Kings Langley is also home to Ovaltine; A. Wander Ltd had their own fleet of narrowboats delivering coal to the works below Langley Lock, and their 'Ovaltine Boats' were renowned for their advertising slogans and colourful paintwork. Preserved Ovaltine motor boat *Albert* may be seen on display at the Batchworth Canal Centre (see page 72). There are several opportunities for a meal: *Millers* pub-restaurant, which has accommodation, the *Rose & Crown* (Benskins) in the High Street serves hot & cold bar food as do *Langleys Steak Bar*, the *Swan* and *Saracen's Head*. There are also Italian and Indian restaurants. A shop, off licence and phone box are to the west and the *Bell* can be found east of Bridge 158.

Bridges 157–162

Passing the mills, weir streams and new red-brick housing (tastefully done) the canal reaches the site of Dickinsons Home Park Mill. Until recently this was a rural stretch, with views along the Gade Valley of pasture, farmland and wooded hillside. Not so today. The M25 crosses on a huge viaduct. Almost obliterated is the

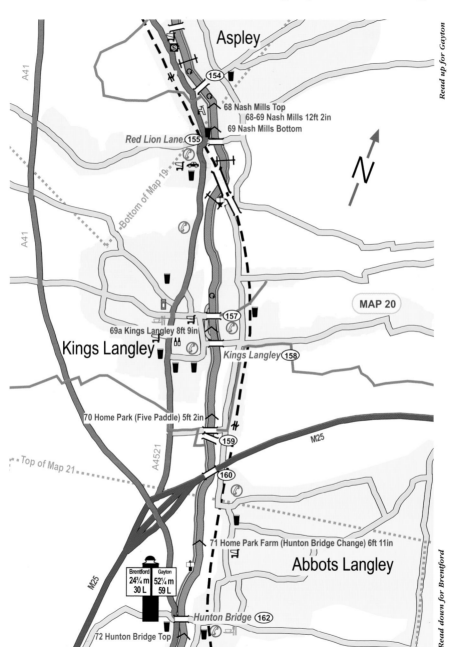

MAP 20
Apsley to Hunton Bridge

Read up for Gayton

Aspley

A41

154

68 Nash Mills Top
68-69 Nash Mills 12ft 2in
69 Nash Mills Bottom

Red Lion Lane 155

Bottom of Map 19

A41

MAP 20

157

69a Kings Langley 8ft 9in

Kings Langley

Kings Langley 158

70 Home Park (Five Paddle) 5ft 2in

159

Top of Map 21

A4521

M25

160

71 Home Park Farm (Hunton Bridge Change) 6ft 11in

Abbots Langley

Brentford	Gayton
24¾ m	52¼ m
30 L	59 L

M25

Hunton Bridge 162

72 Hunton Bridge Top

Read down for Brentford

Euan Corrie

The twisting and landscaped canal past Grove Mill and through Cassiobury Park is spanned by Grove Ornamental Bridge – all provided to placate local landowners whose peace might have been shattered by the new transport artery.

site of a royal hunting lodge, another indication of the regal associations centred on Kings Langley, where relics of a palace and priory remain. Below Lock 71 the Gade re-enters, though it is not easily confused with the main channel.

Hunton Bridge This quiet canalside village is bordered to the north by the well-tended grounds of Rickmansworth Water Works and to the south by Langleybury Park; both fitting preludes. Charles II built a hunting lodge here in 1642, now the _Kings Lodge Restaurant_ (01927 768915). Amazing stucco ceilings depict the arms and insignia of the Royal House of Stewart. For something less formal, the _Kings Head_ is a pleasant pub, offering bar meals (ex Sun eve) and Benskins. There's a children's room and the garden has mooring for patrons. The _Dog & Partridge_ is more the local pub and friendly with it. Bar snacks, pool table and Wed/Fri/Sat discos.

The South West Herts Narrowboat Project is based at Hunton Bridge offering _Dick's Folly_ for hire to "community and youth type groups for the advancement of educational and social welfare". Available to groups of 12 plus leaders. Details from 1 Katherine Close, Hemel Hempstead HP3 9QT (Fax 01992 642465).

Grove Park A series of ornamental bridges mark the canal's passage through Grove Park, once home of the Earls of Clarendon and relatives of the Lords Capel, Earls of Essex who owned Cassiobury Park to the south. Even the A41 and A405 bridges boast decoration. A plaque here honours two men who died during work on the Gade Valley sewer in 1970. Cattle graze the close cropped turf amid stately chestnuts, poplars, oak and ash. This is 'Stubbs' landscape. Lady Capel's Lock is a canal historian's nightmare but most of the dates are not original. The

MAP 21
Hunton Bridge to Cassiobury

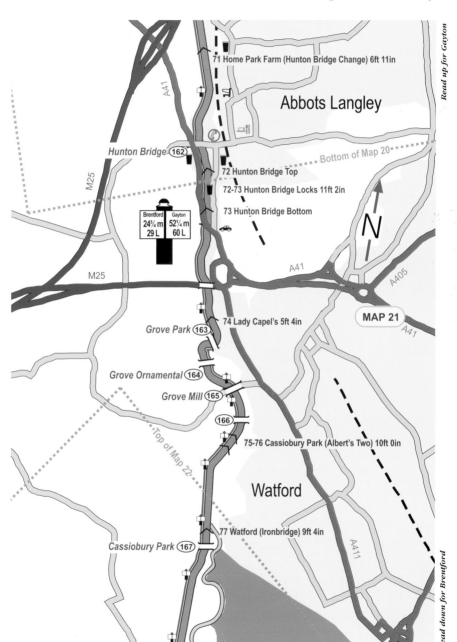

Read up for Gayton

71 Home Park Farm (Hunton Bridge Change) 6ft 11in

Abbots Langley

A41

Hunton Bridge (162)

Bottom of Map 20

M25

72 Hunton Bridge Top

72-73 Hunton Bridge Locks 11ft 2in

73 Hunton Bridge Bottom

N

Brentford	Gayton
24¾ m	52¼ m
29 L	60 L

M25

A41

A405

74 Lady Capel's 5ft 4in

MAP 21

A41

Grove Park (163)

Grove Ornamental (164)

Grove Mill (165)

(166)

Top of Map 22

75-76 Cassiobury Park (Albert's Two) 10ft 0in

Watford

77 Watford (Ironbridge) 9ft 4in

A411

Cassiobury Park (167)

Read down for Brentford

most famous bridge of them all is Grove Ornamental or 'Fancy' bridge, 164. The Earl insisted it be specially built with the towpath on the east bank, and woe betide any boatman who ventured afield! Grove Mill is a rare example of an architect's success: converted to luxury flats, the mill is a perfect complement to the canal, the park and the fascinating array of antiquated machinery which decorates the lawn.

Cassiobury Park In return for their support during the Civil War, the Capel family of Cassiobury were rewarded with the Earldom of Essex. So it was the Earls of Essex and Clarendon (who lived at the Grove) with whom the Grand Junction had to negotiate when they came to settle the route through Watford. The result is one of the most picturesque lengths of canal to be found anywhere in the country. Meandering like a river through 'The Parks', the canal is a Mecca for those who enjoy shaded walks, picnics in the glades and watching boats. The pretty lattice-windowed cottage by Cassiobury Locks has been lovingly restored and Ironbridge Lock is reputedly haunted by a man who keeps opening the bottom gates. This lock too, has another of Cassiobury's ornamented bridges. Cassio Bridge Lock marks the limit of the park, disturbed occasionally by the rumble of passing tube trains.

Bridgewater Basin Watford (01923 211448). Moorings, slipway, hard standing, boat sales & brokerage. Derek Harrison's Amart Services (01296 668186) also operates from here and can deal with boat repairs.

Watford *All services.* One mile east of Bridge 169, this busy town is probably too far away to tempt most people, especially as there are stores just beyond the railway west of Cassio Bridge. There is a Harvester pub by the roundabout at Cassio.

Bridges 169–171

Swinging westwards the canal comes alongside the wasteland that was Dickinson's Croxley Mills, demolished in 1982. The site, now levelled and landscaped, hides a long association with canal transport. The mills received vast quantities of steam coal by boat from their opening in 1830 to the cessation of traffic in 1970.

Croxley Green ⊐🍴 ☕ 🍴 🖋 🛒

Tie up by Common Moor Lock to visit Croxley Green, where there are shops, a station, the *Red House*, the *Coach & Horses*, which serves Greene King and guest ales as well as meals, and the *Artichoke* a walk away up by the Green.

Rickmansworth *All services.*

Sited on the confluence of three rivers, this is a charming old town with much to offer. The long High Street contains many useful shops, a Wetherspoons pub, and the *Fox & Hounds*, a Courage pub which offers food at lunchtimes. There are also an Indian takeaway, kebabs, pizzas, and an Italian Restaurant. The *Coach & Horses*, up the road from the old river Chess wharves serves lunchtime food and Greene King beers.

Three Rivers Museum, which is free and run entirely by volunteers, at 46 High Street, includes displays dealing with local history and the canal as well as having interesting local publications for sale. It is open Mon–Fri afternoons and from 10am to 4pm on Saturdays.

St Mary's Church was extensively rebuilt by the Victorians but early Gothic windows remain. Nearby is the half-timbered vicarage, a brick and timber priory and the Bury.

The Feathers, past the church, has Youngs, Adnams, Bass and guest beers and serves meals (every lunch and all but Sunday eve) and has pub games. The *Whip & Collar* on Uxbridge Road features in the *Good Beer Guide* and offers Adnams, Old Speckled Hen, Fullers and Greene King as well as guest ales and home made meals, especially pies and fish dishes, every lunchtime and evening. It has a pleasant waterside garden.

MAP 22
Cassiobury to Rickmansworth

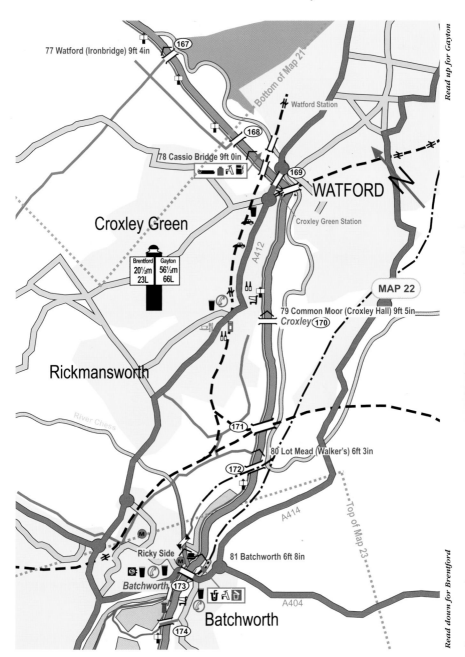

77 Watford (Ironbridge) 9ft 4in

167

Bottom of Map 21

Watford Station

168

78 Cassio Bridge 9ft 0in

169

WATFORD

Croxley Green

Croxley Green Station

A412

Brentford	Gayton
20½m	56½m
23L	66L

MAP 22

79 Common Moor (Croxley Hall) 9ft 5in
Croxley 170

Rickmansworth

River Chess

171

80 Lot Mead (Walker's) 6ft 3in

172

A414

Top of Map 23

M

Ricky Side

M

81 Batchworth 6ft 8in

Batchworth 173

A404

Batchworth

174

Read up for Gayton

Read down for Brentford

Bridge 171 – Batchworth

The tithe barn at Croxley Hall Farm, west of Lot Mead Lock, is the second largest in the country. Below the lock a seemingly endless row of moored boats line the canal – a hotch-potch collection of craft from old working boats to cruisers. These boats crowd round Batchworth Lock and make mooring difficult for the casual visitor, who is advised to take what space he can.

The *White Bear*, is closest

Rickmansworth, looking upstream towards the Cowroast summit. Batchworth Lock and the through route are on the right. To the left, beneath the side bridge is Ricky Side Lock and the river Chess.

south of Bridge 173. The clubhouse of Moor Park Golf Course, set in grounds by Capability Brown, is a huge baroque mansion of 1727 by Leoni and displaying splendid interior frescoes.

River Chess A second lock, Ricky Side Lock, (usually padlocked) at Batchworth links up with the river Chess, a navigable backwater which once served the town wharves, gas works and gravel workings. It includes a rare broad-beam lift bridge and private moorings. A second lock, built in 1903 but now infilled, gave access to the gravel pits.

Batchworth Lock Canal Centre (01923 778382). Alongside the side locks has souvenirs, ices, books and local information including leaflets to guide you on interesting walks around the lakes and canal below Rickmansworth.

'Islanded' between the two locks is *Batchworth Brasserie* which provides light refreshments every weekend in summer. Wooden boats built by Walkers of Rickmansworth, 'Rickys', were built at a timber yard on Frogmoor Wharf, now replaced by a Tesco store.

Stockers Lock The Grand Union is a

schizophrenic canal: at times dull and unspectacular, but at others vibrant and even beautiful. Stocker's Lock is one of its jewels. Three fine buildings, each possessing individual charm, complete a scene of character and unity. Compare the restored lock cottage with its collection of canal artefacts, with the handsome ivy-clad Georgian house beside it. Across the canal the land rises gently to a wooded skyline, Stocker's Farm nestling into a parkland setting of pasture and isolated trees. The blend of materials is, quite unintentionally, almost perfect.

Bridges 175–177

This is a lonely stretch where scars of old industry, quarries and flooded pits oppose lightly wooded farmland like two faces on a coin. A coal Duty Stone stands on the county boundary, marking also the northern limit of Hillingdon's sector of 'Canalway'. The *Whip & Collar*, a Benskins pub, stands beside the A412 ½ mile north-west of Springwell Lock, below which is the Maple Cross Sewage Works, more likely to be remembered for its distinctive aroma than anything else. The Bell Works at Coppermill Lock introduces live industry and some pretty hairy

MAP 23
Rickmansworth

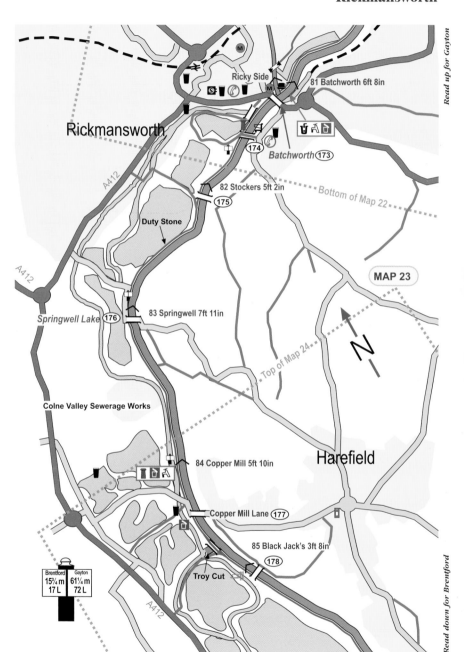

Read up for Gayton

Ricky Side

81 Batchworth 6ft 8in

Rickmansworth

174 Batchworth 173

A412

82 Stockers 5ft 2in
175

Bottom of Map 22

Duty Stone

A412

MAP 23

Springwell Lake 176 83 Springwell 7ft 11in

Top of Map 24

N

Colne Valley Sewerage Works

Harefield

84 Copper Mill 5ft 10in

Copper Mill Lane 177

85 Black Jack's 3ft 8in
178

Troy Cut

A412

Read down for Brentford

	Brentford	Gayton
	15¾ m	61¼ m
	17 L	72 L

turbulence to the canal! It's best to take Bridge 177 at speed to overcome the cross flow from the weir stream, though spare a thought for the canoeists.

Harefield ⊨▐ ▱ ▮▮ ☾ ▯ *Shops*

1 mile south-east of Bridge 177, Harefield is still a village by all accounts, featuring picturesque Elizabethan almshouses and a parish church famed for its monuments. Beside the canal is the *Coy Carp* (01895 821471), A Vintage Inn which serves food all day every day and Tetley or Bass beers. Payphone, children's play area and riverside garden.

Bridges 177–180

A succession of lakes (once sand or gravel pits), watercress beds, meadows and coppice hedgerow are features of the Colne Valley Park, a region of disappearing industry now scheduled for a future in leisure. Landscaping, reclamation and the encouragement of public access are features of a scheme which now sees these flooded gravel pits and their environs used for various recreational pursuits. The Troy Cut, once ¾ mile long, is partially infilled and private, though does offer opportunities for winding.

Black Jack's Lock occupies a chocolate-box setting beside the old corn mill. An Italian restaurant of some repute is housed within (01895 823120/822205 for bookings). Prices seem reasonable but credit cards are not accepted. (Closed Sun eve and Mon). 'Black Jack' dates from very early days and was a Negro employed by a local landowner to harass boatmen passing through at night. Somehow – whether thrown at him or stolen is not clear – he collected a vast number of windlasses before being murdered by an irate victim. The haul was later discovered in the hollow of a nearby tree, but Jack, now with a genuine grudge, still haunts the lock.

A typical Grand Junction Canal Co ground paddle at Stockers Lock.

South Harefield ⊨▐ ▱ ▮▮ ☾ ▯

With little else for several miles either way this is a useful spot to pause for supplies. The *Horse & Barge* serves Fullers, Brakspears and bar food all day every day. There's also a garden. The gravel works here still operate and huge cranes groan and rattle, their grabs eating insatiably. Just below Bridge 180 is the entrance to moorings operated by Harefield Marina, occupying a lagoon formed by the flooding of a long-exhausted gravel pit. In 1958, during the death throes of commercial carrying, 24 working boats were deliberately sunk here, oblivious of the enthusiasts and collectors keen to save them.

Harefield Marina ▬▬ ▮ ⛺ ⚓ ▥ ▯

▮ ♿ ☾ (www.harefieldmarina.co.uk, 01895 822036). Solid fuel, boat sales & brokerage, moorings (permanent and overnight), repairs & servicing, outboard sales & servicing, wetdock, slipway, cranage for cruisers, hard standing, chandlery, books, maps & guides and souvenirs.

Euan Corrie

MAP 24
Harefield to Denham

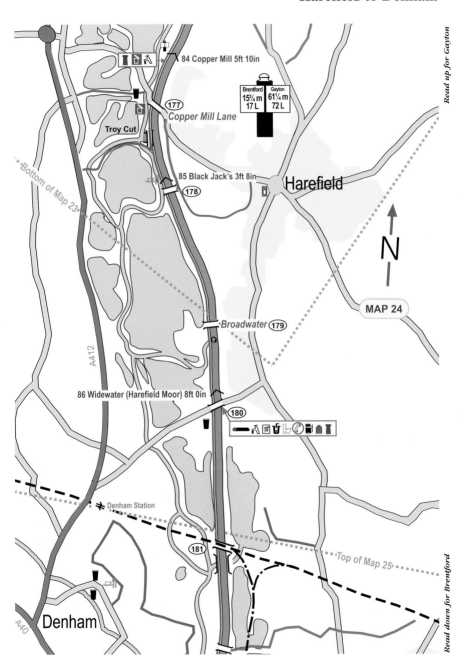

84 Copper Mill 5ft 10in

Brentford	Gayton
15¾ m	61¼ m
17 L	72 L

177 *Copper Mill Lane*

Troy Cut

85 Black Jack's 3ft 8in

178

Harefield

N

MAP 24

Broadwater 179

A412

86 Widewater (Harefield Moor) 8ft 0in

180

Denham Station

181

Denham

A40

Read up for Gayton

Bottom of Map 23

Top of Map 25

Read down for Brentford

Robin Smitbett

An original Grand Junction Canal Co milestone indicating "48 miles to the Thames" survives near Grove Lock although long superceded by the iron plates installed early in the 20th century (below right).

Bridge 180 – Uxbridge

Two long straights, angled at a slight bend connect Harefield and Uxbridge. The route passes Hoveringham Lake, now a sailing base, and is spanned by a handsome, nine-arched blue brick railway viaduct. These are the only breaks in an otherwise featureless landscape.

At 11ft 1in, Denham Deep Lock is the deepest on the Grand Union. It also possesses top gate paddles which will, if opened too soon, flood the well deck of boats resting at the cill. When rising in the lock use ground paddles first and wait for the bows to clear the gate-paddle inlets before opening them. Fran's Tea Garden at the lock cottage (01895 271070) offers teas, coffees and soft drinks. Dogs on leads are welcomed. Open Nov–April 10.30am– 3.30pm (4.30pm on Sun) and 10am–6pm in summer; closed Mondays.

A footbridge crosses the river Colne to follow the Misbourne to Denham village, famous for its film studios. *The Falcon* has home cooked food lunchtime and

evening and caters for those with allergy problems as well as those in search of Brakspear's beers. The river enters the canal within the shade of the A40(M) viaduct, which forms a boundary between rural Colne Valley Park and the townscape of Uxbridge. Cherished back gardens and the Sanderson Fabric's playing fields ease the transition.

As this guide was being prepared news was received of preparations for the first commercial carrying contract on this part of the Grand union Canal since 1980. Wide beam craft now carry aggregates from bridge 183 at Denham to West Drayton so steerers of pleasure craft should remember their obligation to give way to commercial traffic and to watch out for signals that their steerers wish to pass on the wrong side in order to keep to the deepest water.

Denham Day Boats and Denham Boat Services (01895 271070, email: lock87@grandunion.freeserve.co.uk) at Denham Deep Lock, permanent moorings, engine and boat repairs. Day boat hire. Closed Mondays.

Uxbridge *All services, Early Closing Wed.* Though a market town of some age

Euan Corrie

MAP 25
Denham to Uxbridge

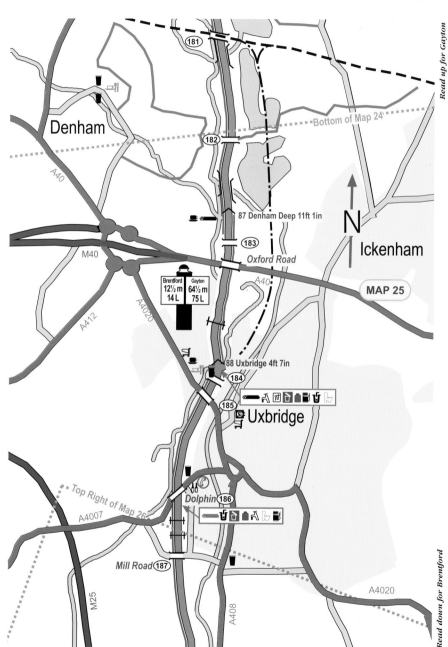

Read up for Gayton

Denham

A40

Bottom of Map 24

181

182

87 Denham Deep 11ft 1in

M40

183

Oxford Road

A40

N

Ickenham

MAP 25

Brentford	Gayton
12½ m	64½ m
14 L	75 L

A412

A4020

88 Uxbridge 4ft 7in

184

185 Uxbridge

Top Right of Map 26

Dolphin 186

A4007

Mill Road 187

M25

A408

A4020

Read down for Brentford

and history, Uxbridge presents a modern face to visitors. There's a Tesco supermarket and a vast shopping complex forms a centrepiece to the town's commercial heart, all the well-known names are here. Perhaps the most interesting building is the *Crown & Treaty Inn* close to Bridge 185. Dating from 1576, the house hosted the Treaty of Uxbridge in February 1645, when representatives of King and Parliament met to discuss an end to the Civil War. Negotiations failed however, though the dispute was finally settled four months later on the battlefield of Naseby. Though the original panelling from the Treaty Room once graced the 78th floor of the Empire State building it has since been returned.

Aside from the *Crown & Treaty* (Wethered's beer and food including Thai cuisine at lunchtime and evenings Mon–Thur as well as all day Fri & Sat) excellent opportunities exist for an evening out. The *Swan & Bottle* is a Chef & Brewer pub by the canal below Uxbridge Lock offering food every lunch time and evening and open all day. Along the A4020 is the *Blue Lagoon* wine bar and restaurant.

Locks 88–89

Uxbridge Lock shrinks beneath the brow of William King's flour mill, now one of the Allied Mills. The lockside is well tended, as are the grounds of Denham Marina & Yacht Station. The twin blocks of the Rank Xerox buildings stand sentry over the canal by Bridge 185, heralding the industry which lies to the south. *The Dolphin*, giving its name to Bridge 186, is a Courage pub with beer garden serving bar meals. The *General Elliott* recalls the defender of Gibraltar in 1792 and has a canalside garden. Uxbridge Boat Centre, opposite, employs the site once used by Fellows, Morton & Clayton, who built and maintained their boats here. Uxbridge Gas Works have been partially dismantled, probably to make way for another industrial estate. The *Lord Hill* nearby is a Courage pub, also with beer garden. Row

upon row of moored boats line the canal continuously from Uxbridge to Cowley. The *Shovel*, once a well-known boatman's pub, now a restaurant, has made boating folk most unwelcome recently. Better, perhaps, to walk to the *Load of Hay* in Villier Street which is *Good Beer Guide* recommended with Crown Buckley Best Bitter and guest ales as well as food (Except Sunday evenings); book at weekends (01895 234676).

Denham Marina Ltd ⌂ ⚓ ⊞ ▣ ◪ ▮ (01895 239811, www.denham-marina.co.uk). Between Bridge 184 and Uxbridge Lock, repairs and maintenance, breakdowns, boatfitting, hard standing, moorings, chandlery, boat sales.

Uxbridge Boat Centre ▬ ⌂ ⚓ ▣ ◪ ▮ (01895 252019, email: ubc@uxbridge99.fsnet.co.uk). Moorings, repairs & maintenance, boatbuilding & fitting, painting, cranage, covered dry dock (to 75ft x 14ft), slipway, DIY facilities, timber, chandlery, gifts, books, maps & guides. Closed Mon. There's a general store and newsagent opposite.

Marine Engine Services (01895 236246, www.marineengine.co.uk) have a workshop at Uxbridge Wharf and offices at Unit 3, 549 Eskdale Road. They are Lister/Petter Marine master distributors and offer vintage engine servicing and advice but will always try to assist callers with engine problems between 8.30 and 5.30 on weekdays.

Cowley ⌑▮ ▭▭ ▦ ▤ ▮

There are shops (one selling gas), takaways and the *Royal Oak* (Benskins and lunches).

Bridges 188–191

Fray's River, a man-made diversion of the Colne, passes under the canal just above Cowley Lock. A sluice beside the chamber was used to empty lock water into the river, as stipulated by the mill owners of Yiewsley. The river was dug to power the

MAP 26
Cowley to Yiewsley

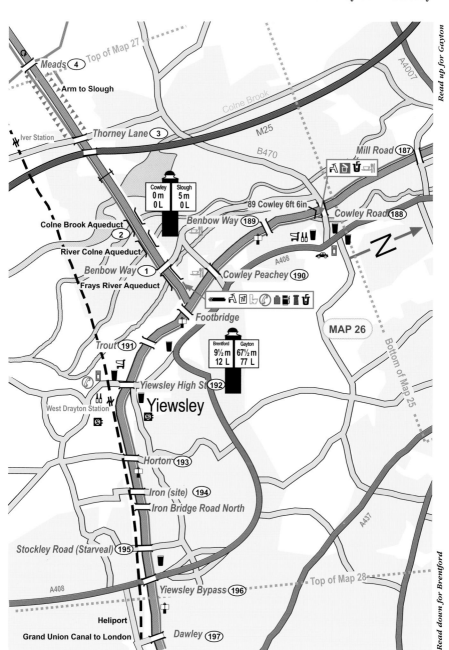

Read up for Gayton

Meads ④

Top of Map 27

Arm to Slough

A4007

Colne Brook

M25

B470

Iver Station

Thorney Lane ③

Mill Road ⑱⑦

Cowley
0 m
0 L

Slough
5 m
0 L

89 Cowley 6ft 6in

Cowley Road ⑱⑧

Colne Brook Aqueduct ②

Benbow Way ⑱⑨

River Colne Aqueduct

A408

Benbow Way ①

Frays River Aqueduct

Cowley Peachey ⑲⓪

Footbridge

MAP 26

Bottom of Map 25

Trout ⑲①

Brentford
9½ m
12 L

Gayton
67½ m
77 L

Yiewsley High St ⑲②

West Drayton Station

Yiewsley

Horton ⑲③

Iron (site) ⑲④

Iron Bridge Road North

A437

Stockley Road (Starveal) ⑲⑤

A408

Yiewsley Bypass ⑲⑥

Top of Map 28

Heliport

Grand Union Canal to London

Dawley ⑲⑦

Read down for Brentford

mills. Cowley Hall Park acts as a floral backdrop in the continuous thread of moored boats lining the canal to Cowley Peachey Junction. Little Britain Country Park, centred on flooded pits, is set aside as a wildlife haven and provides fishing and recreational facilities. The Slough Arm sets off west, straight as a die, and is covered on page 81. The *Jolly Anglers* stands back from the canal at Bridge 191.

Cowley Peachey

A mainly residential area deriving its name from the Pecche family who owned the manorial rights in the 13th century. The *Paddington Packet Boat* (Fullers) commemorates the famous passenger services inaugurated in 1801. The 'packet' ran from here to Paddington, pulled by four horses and completing the 20 mile journey in around 6 hours. The pub serves bar food Mon–Sat lunch and welcomes families. Up on the main road near the top of Packet Boat Lane are shops and a laundrette. The *Turning Point* stands by the canal at Bridge 190. Beyond the Frays river from this bridge on Old Mill Lane is *Quackers Restaurant* where denim is out but cabaret and dancing are in, Thur–Sat. Booking is advised (01895 237559) especially if wanting admission for children to eat.

British Waterways, Cowley Peachey Marina 🛏 🅰 ⛽ 📶 (www. britishwaterways.co.uk, 01895 449851). Open 9am–5.30pm weekdays.

High Line Yachting 🅰 🔌 🛢 🔋 ⚓ (01753 651496, www.highline.co.uk) provide the majority of services at Cowley Peachey Marina. Repairs and maintenance, boatfitting and steelwork, moorings, covered (and heated) wetdock, boat painting, brokerage, Boat Safety inspections, call outs, coal. The shop sells chandlery, souvenirs, open Tue–Sat. High Line Yachting also operate from Iver on the Slough Arm and premises on the Paddington Arm.

Yiewsley and West Drayton

All services. The canal keeps the two towns apart and probably represents the only scenic attraction for either. Towards West Drayton is the *De Burgh Arms*; a Taylor Walker house with guest beers and a la carte restaurant (ex Sun eve bookings: 01895 442018), pool table and payphone. The De Burghs owned the manor here, and part of a 16th century gateway can still be seen. The church contains some fine monuments and a 15th century font. There are several pubs, takeaways and late shopping at the Co-op. The *Brickmakers Arms* is north of Bridge 193.

Bridges 192–196

A mix of industry and wasteland, though 325 acres of Stockley Park have been earmarked for recreation and a science park. However, granted that rural landscape, with the occasional village and well presented town is the ideal, there is still enjoyment to be had from industrial sectors, which, though unkempt, are rarely tedious. This stretch is no exception: note the Slimcea factory competing with one of two vast scrapyards. The Yiewsley by-pass crosses by the *Foresters*, a Courage pub. Amey Roadstone have a huge cement works here and behind it is the old Broad's Dock, long since truncated by the railway but worth preserving for its wildlife.

Grand Union Main Line south to Brentford continues on page 84, Map 28.

Introduction

There's a real sense of achievement to be gained by cruising the length of this arm. The round trip need only take 3½ hours. The Slough Arm was one of the last canals to be built in Britain, being completed as late as 1882. Its purpose was to serve the gravel pits and brickworks developing around the western limits of London which later, as the pits were exhausted, became the refuse tip for the bustling Victorian metropolis. Though commercial traffic has ceased, the arm is recognised as a valuable recreational amenity and, when the last 1½ miles was threatened by a new road scheme, fierce local opposition increased awareness of its potential. In 1974 it was upgraded to 'Cruiseway' status, and though the Slough Canal Group has been disbanded, credit must go to their efforts. In the early 1970s a realistic proposition to extend the arm to the Thames at Windsor was rejected, surprisingly, by Slough Council. Many visitors may be interested by the extensive and varied wildlife which thrives along the canal banks, especially the rare and unusual plants. These are said to stem from sweepings dumped here from London's markets years ago. The towpath is very popular with walkers, joggers, anglers and bounty hunters, the latter searching for pot lids and discarded Victoriana, the result of tipping refuse brought in trains of wide boats from London around the turn of the century.

From Cowley Peachey Junction

Head out for Slough in early evening and you could be rewarded by a beautiful sunset, reflected in the still waters that stretch away straight as a laser's beam for almost 2½ miles. Three sizeable aqueducts on this first stretch cross the Fray's River, Colne and Colne Brook. Each very similar, they consist of a simple iron trough with lattice railings, painted black with white capping, and brick abutments. In common with the canal's bridges, which are generally either of grey brick or iron, they are typical of the late 'railway age', being large and robust, yet attaining a functional practicality that is not without merit. The flooded gravel pits of Little Britain Country Park lend a rural aspect. The same cannot be said of the M25, which strides over the canal on a severe

Setting out onto the railway-age straightness of the Slough Arm.

Euan Corrie

concrete viaduct. The towpath is walkable but can be below par, especially past Iver.

High Line Yachting ⚓ ⛽ 📷 🅿 🛢 🪣 ⚓

Mansion Lane, Iver (01753 651496). Repairs & maintenance, breakdowns (9am–6pm), boatfitting and steel work, hard standing, moorings, cranage, slipway and gantry, brokerage and insurance, showers. The shop sells chandlery and souvenirs. A brass plaque is available here to those who can show evidence of having navigated the arm to Slough.

Iver *Most services, station.* ½ mile south of the canal. This residential dormitory town for London has some handsome Georgian buildings, including Bridgefoot House, and the old church contains some interesting monuments and a fine 12th century chancel. There are several pubs, notably the *Bull* and the *Oddfellows*, which serve lunches, the *Fox & Pheasant* and the *Swan,* which has a restaurant.

Rooftops of the Ridgeway Trading Estate and Langley's industrial outskirts keep a respectful distance from the canal, but beware of the inhabitants of the squalid shanty town by Hollow Hill Lane, and their ill-disciplined dogs!

Langley

More worked-out gravel pits and light industry herald Langley. By the station is the *Willow Tree*, a Courage pub serving home-cooked food and there's a farm shop by Langley Station Bridge. The commercial centre is south of the station but old Langley is nearer the Schools and Trenches bridges. The *Red Lion* is a cheerful olde-worlde pub near the church where you can drink Courage beers and enjoy a lunchtime snack. The *Chestnuts*, closer to the canal, serves lunches (ex Sat & Sun) and Courage beers. There's a payphone, garden and pool table.

To Slough

As one approaches Slough, houses and industry begin to encroach, though market gardening and greenhouses do not offend. The water is generally very clear but may be choked by weeds in summer. The last bend opens out to reveal the final dead straight mile. At Slough the canal ends! It can hardly be said to be a terminus, just a road and some houses in the way. In fact there is plenty of room to wind, evidence of a loading wharf and a mooring ring. From the landsman's point of view an insignificant sign indicates "canal towpath". What a contrast to the activity of a hundred years ago. The *Nags Head* (Courage) is just over the road from the basin and has been extensively rebuilt. They do lunches (ex Sun) and have a payphone. Near the shops of Wrexham Road Bridge is the *Tanners*, which serves good lunches (a la carte & basket meals, ex Sun) in pleasant surroundings.

Slough *All services, Early Closing Wed, Market Day Tues. A&E at Wexham Park Hospital Wexham Street*, but always dial 999 first in an emergency. This large modern, and heavily industrial town has never really recovered its public esteem since the late Sir John Betjeman gave it a pasting with the words 'Come, friendly bombs, and fall on Slough, it isn't fit for humans now'! The trading estate is one of the largest in the country and many household names, Mars, Johnson & Johnson and Commodore among them, have their origins here. Slough does have a history though, being centred on the old town of Upton. The planet Uranus was first discovered here by William Herschel . . . using a telescope of course, and he lies in St Lawrence's churchyard amid the yews, reputedly the inspiration for Gray's Elegy. Upton Court next to the Norman church dates from the 16th century. The town lies south from the Wharf and there's an Information Centre on Bath Road.

For Grand Union Main Line north to Gayton go to page 80 and Map 26. For Grand Union Main Line south to Brentford go to page 84, Map 28.

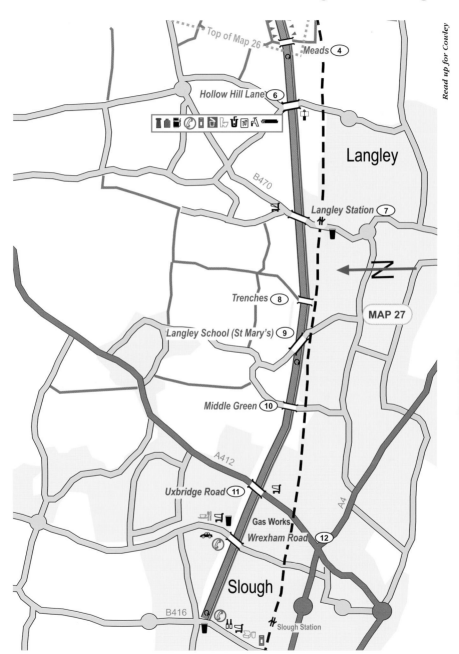

MAP 27

Slough Arm – Slough

Read up for Cowley

Top of Map 26

Meads (4)

Hollow Hill Lane (6)

Langley

B470

Langley Station (7)

N

Trenches (8)

MAP 27

Langley School (St Mary's) (9)

Middle Green (10)

A412

A4

Uxbridge Road (11)

Gas Works

Wrexham Road (12)

Slough

B416

Slough Station

For **Grand Union Main Line** north to Gayton go to page 80 and Map 26.

Bridges 196–199

The towpath opposite the heliport and through Dawley cutting is permanently soggy, but an old timber yard by Bridge 198 offers good moorings for those visiting the *Woolpack*, a Courage pub with an unusual tiled bar. Food, garden, payphone and pool table.

Hayes *All Services.* No longer a village but an important industrial and residential area of west London. Of interest are the factories of Walls and Nestlé – the smell of coffee can be quite strong. Access is good at Bridge 200, where there are shops, pubs, laundrette and a bank. The *Blue Anchor* by Bridge 199 faces Dunlop across the canal. It serves Fullers, Ruddles and Combes, and has a restaurant (every lunch, plus Thu–Sat eves; breakfast Sun–Fri), payphone and garden.

Bridge 200 – Bull's Bridge

Crossing Yeading Brook on a small aqueduct, itself crossed by a new bypass, the canal passes between Hillingdon and Ealing/Southall. 'Canalway' plaques mark the boundary.

Bull's Bridge 🛈 ⚓

The Paddington Arm of the Grand Union Canal meets the main line at Bull's Bridge. The site was an important maintenance centre for 200 years and BW had a major depot here. Controversially almost all the facilities were cleared to make way for a Tesco supermarket in the mid 1990s. There is a laundrette along the main road from the supermarket entrance. Just south of the junction is the lay-by where the GUCCCo had a fuel and supply depot for their fleet of some 120 pairs of narrowboats. There are emotive photographs of the fleet gathered here in the 1930s awaiting orders. In stark contrast, it is used today for moorings and filled with houseboats, mostly of the float-

For **Paddington Arm** see page 92, Map 30.

Bull's Bridge lay-by in the early 1950s. Working boats wait for cargoes where houseboats are now moored.

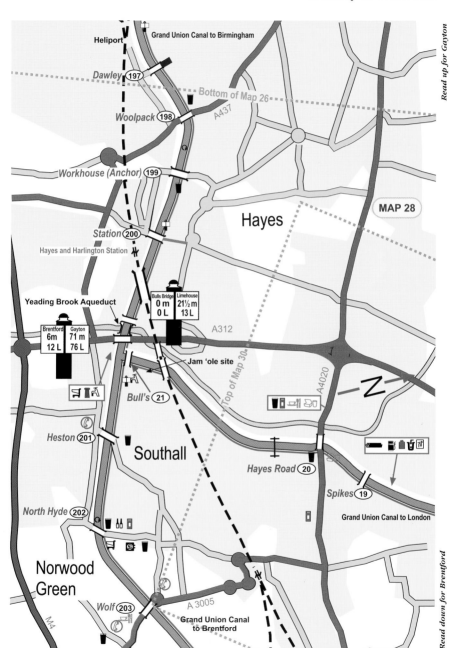

MAP 28
Dawley to Norwood

Read up for Gayton

Heliport

Grand Union Canal to Birmingham

Dawley (197)

Bottom of Map 26

A437

Woolpack (198)

Workhouse (Anchor) (199)

Hayes

MAP 28

Station (200)

Hayes and Harlington Station

Yeading Brook Aqueduct

Bulls Bridge	Limehouse
0 m	21½ m
0 L	13 L

Brentford	Gayton
6m	71 m
12 L	76 L

A312

Jam 'ole site

A4020

Z

Bull's (21)

Heston (201)

Southall

Hayes Road (20)

Spikes (19)

North Hyde (202)

Grand Union Canal to London

Norwood
Green

Wolf (203)

A 3005

Grand Union Canal
to Brentford

M4

Read down for Brentford

ing 'mobile home' variety. The *Grand Junction Arms,* one of three on the canal, is canalside at Bridge 201. It's open all day and serves food noon to 7pm Mon–Thur and at weekend lunchtimes and has a pool table and canalside garden.

Bridges 201–203

This is a largely residential stretch, bordered by housing, gardens and only light industry. Take care though as rubbish can be a hazard here. Beside Bridge 202 is the *Old Oak Tree* (Courage) with its big screen TV. Opposite a large timber yard is Adelaide Dock.

Norwood Green 🍷 🍴 🍽 ☕

Shops. This is useful mooring spot for those taking a breather either before or after Hanwell and Norwood locks. New housing overlooks the canal and the air is busy with 'planes; Heathrow Airport being only 4 miles south west. Though the pub standing beside Bridge 203 is the *Lamb* (an amenable pub open all day for London Pride and Guinness with moorings and canalside garden) the bridge earns its name from the *Wolf,* which is some 200 yards south. It welcomes travellers, offering Youngs, Adnams and London Pride, bar lunches and evening meals Mon–Sat plus Sunday lunches (020 8574 5775). There is a laundrette and Post Office opposite.

Bridges 203–204

A dead-straight mile ends at Norwood Top Lock, where there are BW facilities and a café. Maypole Dock heads off north and is private, having been built in 1912 to serve the Monsted margarine works. It is used for moorings.

British Waterways Norwood Top Lock 🛠 📶 (020 8571 8902, see also page 15). The local waterway manager's office (open: 8.30am to 5pm Mon–Fri) is alongside Norwood Top Lock and is a good source for details of boat licences and moorings, fishing and other canalside activities.

Bridges 204–208

Norwood Locks mark the southern limit of the lock-free length bounded by Camden, Slough and Cowley, known to boatmen as 'the long level'. Windmill (205) or 'Three Bridges', is a unique site where road, rail and water meet and cross in a simultaneous tangle of bridges and cuttings. With Heathrow so close there is the interesting possibility of all four principal transport modes passing vertically one above another!

Hanwell The red-brick lock cottage at Hanwell Top faces the long wall of St Bernard's Hospital across the lock, and the flight is generally spruce and tidy, though side ponds don't work. A BW key is required to release the paddles. Set into the hospital wall are the little red doors used by firemen to gain access to the canal waters, while horse steps built into the towpath near the middle lock allowed horses, dragged into the canal on the tight bend, to clamber out again. Coal deliveries were made to the hospital via a short arm next to Lock 94, which gained the name 'Asylum Lock' from the association. At the foot of the flight the river Brent enters and a footpath heads off westward to Osterley Park. The river is navigable, unofficially, at least, as far as Hanwell Bridge, but winding for craft in excess of 35ft will be difficult. The area is designated the Brent River Park and much landscaping has been done. *The Fox* is a Free House offering Timothy Taylor's Landlord, London Pride and Brakspears beers as well as home-cooked lunches every day. There are shops in nearby Hanwell and the *Dolphin* on Lower Boston Road serves meals every lunchtime and evening except Monday with Brakspears, Fullers and Marstons beers. Industry returns around Ontario Bridge. A plaque here commemorates the winning of the Kerr Cup for pile-driving by the local maintenance gang in 1959.

Osterley Park & House ¾ mile south west. A fine mansion built in 1576 altered in 1711 and lavishly redecorated by

It comes as a surprise to find that Gallows Bridge was cast at the Horsley Ironworks, more usually associated with the Birmingham Canals, but in fact this may have been their first canal structure.

Robert Adam in 1763–67. The house – now administered by the National Trust – contains some exceptional tapestries, paintings and furniture and is open from April to November on Weds–Suns & Bank Hols 1pm–4.30pm, (01494 755597.) The Park is open 9am–7.30pm.

Osterley Lock cottage has been demolished but refurbishment nearby has resulted in a new footbridge and intriguing toothed weir. The weir is set back and unlikely to pose problems except under exceptional circumstances, such as those prevalent in June 1903 when heavy rains closed the canal for several weeks!

The Piccadilly Line clatters over by Wyke Green Golf course almost within sight of Gallows Bridge, believed to be the first canal bridge by Horseley Ironworks. Though carrying the slogan; 'Grand Union Canal Co 1820', the GU wasn't formed until 1929 and closer examination reveals an obscured 'Junction' beneath the 'Union'. The elevated M4 sweeps round to join the Great West Road.

Boston Manor A charming three-storey Tudor mansion with Jacobean additions, dating from 1622; including historic furniture and local paintings. Open April–Oct weekends & bank holidays only (020 8583 4535, www.cip.org.uk). Park open daily all year.

Bridge 208 – The Thames

Brentford depot was formerly a very busy place for water transport. Here, for many years, cargoes were transhipped from river lighters, towed by tugs from ships in London's docks, to narrowboats for onward transport to the Midlands, etc, via the Grand Union Canal.

In the 1970s and 80s, with the virtual disappearance of the narrowboat fleets, the lighterage traffic was transhipped direct to road transport or into the warehouses for storage. At the time of writing only one warehouse remains, close to the London & South Western Railway bridge at the top of the dock, and the whole of the island between the canal and the river Brent backwater is being swamped with new apartment buildings. At up to £½m each you'll need an extra £8,000 for a car parking permit so it's probably best to arrive by boat! The towpath, at all times excellent, passes within the cavernous expanse of the last covered dock and there is much to entertain the walker. At the head of the locks the former Fellows, Morton & Clayton Dock almost survives, although the developers felt obliged to reduce the water area of even this miniature arm in order to pack in the maximum new housing.

Brentford Gauging Locks, paired, are no longer manned and were once the point where traffic joining the canal from the Thames or loaded nearby was assessed for tolls. Hopefully the listed Toll House will survive the changes all around. You will need your BW yale key to gain access to the powered lock operating mechanism on the island between the chambers. Beyond, overlooking the Brent, stands the Boatman's Institute of 1904, now a private house. Below Bridge 209 the towpath is intermittent and access awkward, though it can be rejoined via the Ham, Brent Way, Boars Head Yard or

Euan Corrie

All the craft loading at Brentford and those heading up the canal off the Thames were 'gauged' in lock 100 when a clerk measured the tonnage aboard. Alongside the Gauging Locks the office built for these clerks and their tonnage tables still survives but when we were researching this guide its surroundings were in the throes of total redevelopment.

Dock Road. Thames Locks are also paired and are manned, set amid a confusion of backwaters, docks, yards and wharves. The pound above is partly tidal; that part below totally so, joining the river Thames opposite Kew Gardens.

Brentford Marine (Ridgeway Motors) (020 8560 6561) Brent Way. Moorings. Repairs.

SPL Marine at Thames Lock Wharf on Dock Road, (020 8560 9326, www.splmarine.com) reached via the backwater from Brentford Creek are open from 8am–5pm Mon–Fri, but only by appointment at weekends. There is a slipway, a tidal grid and a drydock which are used for repairs, building and conversions of substantial boats and barges. Chandlery is available.

Brentford *All services. Laundrette.* (Hounslow Tourist Information Centre 020 8583 2929).

While you wait for the tide there is plenty to occupy your time in this ancient market town, once capital of Middlesex. Julius Caesar first crossed the Thames here in

MAP 29
Norwood to Brentford

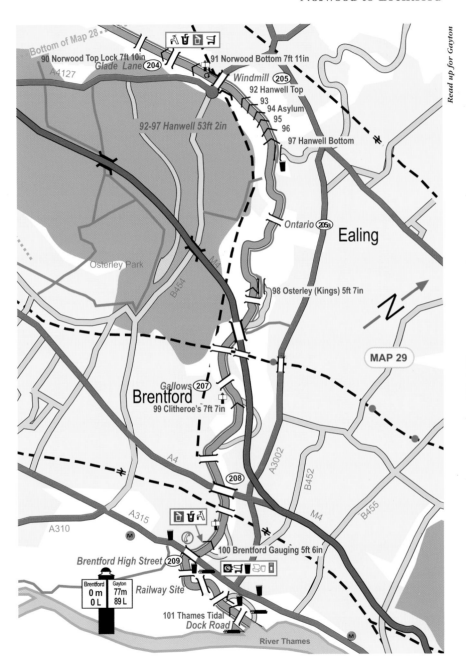

Read up for Gayton

Bottom of Map 28

90 Norwood Top Lock 7ft 10in
Glade Lane (204)
A4127

91 Norwood Bottom 7ft 11in

Windmill (205)
92 Hanwell Top
93
94 Asylum
95
96
97 Hanwell Bottom

92-97 Hanwell 53ft 2in

Ontario (206a) **Ealing**

98 Osterley (Kings) 5ft 7in

Osterley Park

B454
M4

MAP 29

Gallows (207)
Brentford
99 Clitheroe's 7ft 7in

A4
A3002
B452
B455

(208)

A315
A310
M4

Brentford High Street (209)

100 Brentford Gauging 5ft 6in

Brentford	Gayton
0 m	77m
0 L	89 L

Railway Site

101 Thames Tidal
Dock Road

River Thames

54BC, probably over the sand bar formed by the river Brent, later known as 'Brent ford'. 150 yards west of Bridge 209 is the entrance to Syon Park (open daily, (020 8560 0882, www.syonpark.co.uk), where there is a garden centre, butterfly house (020 8560 7272), and the famous Heritage Collection of British motor cars (ex Mon). The house, which is considered one of Adam's finest, is also open Apr–Oct: from 11am–5pm Wed, Thur, and Sun. The Gardens are open daily from 10.30am–5.30pm. Opened in 1984 is the Brentford Waterman's Arts Centre, opposite Lots Ait, which houses a theatre, cinema, gallery and workshop, as well as a bar and restaurant (020 8586 1176). Head for Kew Bridge and you will pass the Musical Museum at 368 High Street. Open Mar–Oct weekends it contains a fascinating collection of mechanical and unusual musical instruments from music boxes to a Wurlitzer organ (020 8560 8108). Housed in the old Grand Junction Waterworks Co pumping station is the Kew Bridge Steam Museum, a living steam museum open daily and in steam Sat, Sun and Bank Hols (020 8568 4757, www.kbsm.org.uk). There are excellent displays explaining water treatment and distribution in London. The company's name is indeed confirmation that the original supplies came from the canal at Paddington but eventually the source was transferred to the works at Kew in a search for improved quality. The majestic action of the 90 inch Cornish Beam Engine, steamed on weekend afternoons, should not be missed. Across the river lies the Royal Botanic Gardens (open daily 020 8332 5655, www.kew.org.uk); Kew Palace (open daily Apr–Sept); the Queen's Cottage (open weekends Apr–Sept) and various museums. Gunnersbury Park, north of Kew Bridge, contains an early 19th century house built by the Rothschilds, now a museum (open daily, afternoons, 020 8992 1612).

Euan Corrie

The Boatmen's Mission building still survives, in private ownership, at Brentford.

Eating & Drinking Brentford's most famous waterway pub is the *Brewery Tap* (Fullers) in Catherine Wheel Road, just up from Thames Locks. This friendly dockland-style pub serves lunches, snacks (Sat lunch) and evening meals and there's live jazz on Thurs. Other pubs near the canal include, to the west, the *Northumberland Arms*, a free house offering bar lunches Mon–Fri and the *George & Dragon* (Charringtons & bar meals, ex Sun), while to the east are the *Six Bells* (meals & live music), the *Beehive* (Fullers and meals) and the *Magpie & Crown* (changing real ales and ciders). Various shops and services in the High Street including a Tandoori Rrestaurant.

Navigational Procedures

Vessels passing between the canal and the river Thames (above Teddington Lock) MUST have the appropriate licences. To navigate the Thames above Teddington Lock requires registration **in advance** from The Environment Agency, Kings Meadow House, Kings Meadow Road, Reading RG1 8DQ. (0118-9535 5525) (long- or short-term licences.) Likewise, boats entering the canal at Brentford must be licensed with British Waterways. This may also be achieved in advance or on arrival at Thames Lock, Brentford. Proof of the possession of a current Boat Safety Certificate and third party insurance cover will be required. The tidal Thames to Teddington falls within the jurisdiction of the Port of London Authority and details regarding tides and moorings can be obtained from the address on page 15.

As the Thames at Brentford is tidal it is possible to enter the canal only at certain times. Thames Lock (101) is manned but entrance may be made only during the period from 2hrs before to 2hrs after high water, between 6am–10pm. (High water may be calculated by adding approx. 1 hr to the times published for London Bridge.) Before attempting a passage either way it is essential to check with BW by telephoning 020 8568 2779 preferably at least 24hrs beforehand. (A comprehensive timetable for the availability of these and London's other tidal locks is available from any BW office in the London area, see page 15, or from the keepers at Teddington Lock.)

The Gauging Locks (100) are operated by boat crews who will need a BW Yale key to access the mechanism.

Thames-bound skippers are best advised to wait at Brentford Pool, where access is easier, and aim to join the river on the rising tide, so aiding their passage upstream to Teddington (Lock keeper: 020 8940 8728). Those aiming to join the canal really ought to stay at Teddington until they can be sure of an unhindered passage, ideally leaving there at high water and using the ebb to pass clear through Richmond Tidal barrier rather than using the lock and arrive at Brentford Creek 1–1½hrs later. Those making for Brentford from the Lower Thames, either from Limehouse or Bow Creek, should make best use of the rising tide to reach Brentford Creek before it turns. If you do arrive early, or when the locks are closed, anchor off the Surrey Bank (Kew) away from any barge traffic. Check for depth of water, beware of shoals and allow adequate depth at low tide.

It is compulsory for boats over 66ft (20m) navigating the tidal Thames to carry VHF radio (see page 112).

Obey the lock keepers at all times and observe speed limits: 4mph on the canal, 3mph on the river. (NB. At exceptionally high water headroom may be restricted under Dock Road and Brentford bridges). If you are in any doubt, telephone!

Boaters planning a round-London waterway tour by canal and river are advised that it is best to proceed down the Regent's Canal to Limehouse Basin and up the Thames to Brentford on the flood tide – rather than the other way round.

Bull's Bridge

The turn is not awkward, unlike some, but all the traditional features of a canal junction are here: stop gates, toll office, roving bridge but the maintenance depot has vanished under the supermarket. A motley collection of barges has been abandoned in the wide between here and the railway bridge and several infilled arms can be discerned. These include Tickler's Dock, the famous 'Jam 'Ole'. Tickler's made the jam but most cargoes went to Kearly & Tonge, biscuit manufacturers whose coal deliveries finished in 1970 and were the last regular long-distance traffic on the canal. This next section is being redeveloped, with the Southall gas works standing isolated among the debris. The gasometers still dominate and the land is barren and desolate. West of the Uxbridge Road (Bridge 20) EMI have their record distribution centre and Wimpey an office complex.

Southall *All services, Early Closing Wed.* Tourist Information Centre, Perceval House, 16 Uxbridge Road, Ealing, (www.ealing.gov.uk/tourism, 020 8280 1000). ¾ mile south, the town has a good shopping centre, though smaller outlets are strung along the A4020. The *Hamborough Tavern* offers hot & cold bar lunches and evening meals (ex Sun) and serves Ruddles and Yorkshire Bitter. There's a take-away close by too.

Bridges 20–18

The newer premises near Bridge 20 illustrate well the changing attitude towards our waterways, with lawns, conifers and bench seats encouraging a lunchtime audience of office staff. The open parkland and rough pasture to the north was once Hayes Brickfield and until recently a major tip for city rubbish, once an important traffic on the canal. Some of the wharves remain, providing easy moorings for the casual visitor, and a graceful single-span concrete footbridge links the new park with housing to the east.

Willowtree Marina 🛟 🚿 📮 🅿 🛒 🛠 🔧 🏪 🏬 🅿 ⓒ Close to Bridge 19 (020 8841 6585, www.willowtreemarina.co.uk). Visitor and permanent moorings, showers, laundrette, trailboat slipway, Boat Safety Scheme inspections, restaurant. Open 9.15am–4.30pm every day. B&Q and Tesco are very handy by the marina access road.

The *Quayside Bistro* (020 8841 2500; email: quaysidebistro@tesco.net) is at Willowtree Marina and is open at lunchtime and evening Mon–Fri as well as all day Sun serving John Smiths beers and a wide range of wines with an á la carte menu specialising in Mediterranean cuisine.

Greenford The town centre is a long walk (1 mile east) but the *Civil Engineer* is close to Bridge 18 (Courage, hot & cold lunches). The name honours the pub's famous neighbour, Taylor Woodrow, whose offices straddle the canal.

High Line Yachting 🛟 🚿 📮 🅿 🏪 🏬 🅿 ⓒ

Northolt (020 8845 9924, www.highline.co.uk) Coal, moorings (including residential), hard standing, engine and boat repairs, fitting out, painting and brokerage, showers, postbox. Open Tue–Fri 9am–6pm, Sat 9am–5pm.

Northolt 🍴 🛒

Northolt Aerodrome, with its Spitfire and Polish War Memorial, is a long way from Northolt village, itself ½ mile north of Bridge 16. There are two churches, shops and pubs.

Bridges 16–14

This is an interesting stretch with many household names to tick off as you pass. A gentle 'S'-bend leads into the lengthy straight that passes Lyons and Tetley's. The Lyons Dock was the last to be built on the Paddington Arm (in 1926) and still looks remarkably fresh and new. There's an appetising smell of coffee in the air and Lyons Maid have made commendable

MAP 30

Paddington Arm – Southall to Northolt

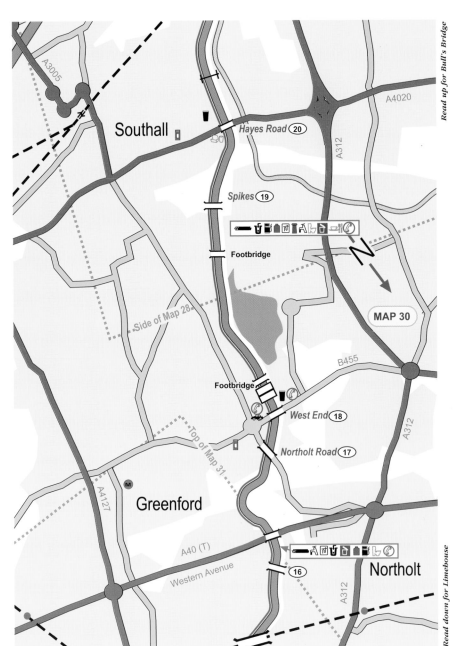

Read up for Bull's Bridge

Southall

Hayes Road ⓏⓄ

A4020

A312

Spikes ⑲

Footbridge

Side of Map 28

N

MAP 30

B455

Footbridge

West End ⑱

A312

Northolt Road ⑰

Top of Map 31

Greenford

A4127

Ⓜ

A40 (T)

Western Avenue

Northolt

A312

Read down for Limehouse

efforts at landscaping their frontage with conifers and decorative shrubs. At Black Horse Bridge is the pub of that name, a Fullers house open all day with extensive garden and offering lunches Mon–Fri. South of Bridge 15 beyond the A40 is the London Motorcycle Museum, which is open at weekends. A series of tight bends twist between Mother's Pride and Glaxo and the canal straightens in the middle of Sudbury Golf Course.

Bridges 14–12

Coppiced Horsenden Hill rises up to a 277ft summit, affording fine views in all directions. Beyond the towpath is Perivale Wood, a 27 acre refuge for the remains of ancient Middlesex Forest. Oak, hazel and shrubs harbour a rich variety of birds and flora. The site is managed by the Selborne Society who hold an open day in early May (usually 2nd Sun).

Willowtree Narrowboat Trips

Operate from Horsenden Hill Visitor Centre, close to Ballot Box Bridge (13) providing public trips on Wednesdays, Sundays and Bank Holidays in summer with food available if pre-booked. Full boat charter for up to 40 people is also available with a variety of catering options. (020 8841 2100)

Alperton *All services.*

With good moorings and services, including Sainsburys and B&Q, this is a useful spot to pause for provisions. There are shops, pubs and take-aways in all directions and the friendly *Pleasure Boat* (Taylor Walker) beside Bridge 11 offers hot food Mon–Fri, payphone and moorings. A special treat is to find the Royal Bengal sweet shop. If you've never tried Indian sweets then here's your chance. Pick a selection as they're all delicious.

Bridge 11 – North Circular Aqueduct

The new 'tube' bridge links industry with housing, and Stonebridge Park includes canal-conscious factories, although steer-

ers will probably be concentrating more on their approach to the North Circular Aqueduct. It comes as an anti-climax. The present twin aqueduct structure was built in 1993, replacing that of 1930 to accommodate widening of the North Circular Road which passes beneath it.

Navigation Note In common with many other pounds on the southern Grand Union this one, stretching for 25 miles between Camden and Slough, has been lowered by BW to combat seepage. The drop, of only a few inches, has nevertheless generated problems. Wash damage from passing boats has been accentuated and steerage impaired by reduced depth, while mooring is frequently impossible.

Park Royal A grand name for a prestigious industrial site. During WWI the Park Royal munitions factories kept the guns blazing across the trenches and, once established as a major trading estate, the famous names moved in. Heinz arrived in 1925, followed by Guinness, both using the canal to bring in raw materials. The tiny canal cottage splitting a garage in two was built in 1830, and is now listed.

Bridges 10–8

Industrial sections are rarely pretty but they are interesting. Heinz' extensive frontage offers a fascinating panorama of activity, with sights and smells to intrigue. The feeder from Brent Reservoir enters by the fire station and boats up to 45ft should be able to turn here. The keen eyed will pick out the McVities factory but you'll have to be very short-sighted to miss Acton Lane Power Station. Built in 1945, it uses canal water for cooling and, until the late 50s, received coal by canal.

Harlesden ¼ mile north east. Certainly worth stopping for is the *Grand Junction* (Youngs) by Bridge 9. There are bar meals, hot snacks and regular barbecues in the summer (no food Sun). Moorings, canal-side terrace, children's play area, facilities for the disabled and live entertainment in the garden in summer.

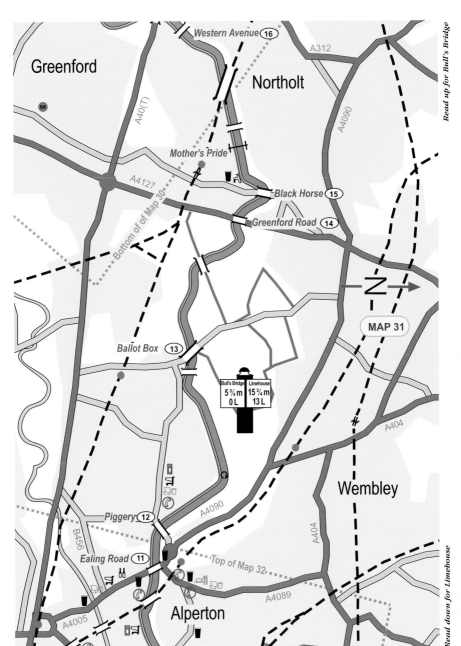

MAP 31
Paddington Arm – Northolt to Alperton

Read up for Bull's Bridge

Greenford

Western Avenue 16

A312

Northolt

A40(T)

A4090

Mother's Pride

A4127

Black Horse 15

Greenford Road 14

Bottom of Map 30

N

MAP 31

Ballot Box 13

Bull's Bridge | Limehouse
5¾ m | 15¾ m
0 L | 13 L

A404

Wembley

A4090

Piggery 12

B456

A404

Ealing Road 11

Top of Map 32

A4089

A4005

Alperton

Read down for Limehouse

Bridge 8–5

A grassy cutting keeps the view of industry at bay, though a recurring net of railway lines is a constant reminder of nearby Willesden Freightliner Terminal. The huge Walls meat factory is hard to miss too. Willesden Junction Station is convenient at Old Oak, where you'll also find the *Fisherman's Arms*.

The towpath from Acton Lane has been laid with power lines by the CEGB and concrete slabs carrying dire warnings about voltages protect the cables from errant mooring stakes. Heard, but not seen, behind the towpath wall is the former Great Western Railway on a lower level to the canal. By Mitre Bridge (6) is the modern North Pole International Depot where Eurostar Channel Tunnel trains are serviced.

Quite suddenly, everything opens out and there's Wormwood Scrubs. Look over the towpath and you'll see London spread way before you. Pick out the Post Office Tower, White City (that was), Wormwood Scrubs Prison, Queens Park Rangers Football Club ground, BBC Television Centre and many more. In contrast, on the opposite bank is the tranquillity and seclusion of Kensal Green Cemetery. It's worth stopping to wander round the elaborate headstones, monuments and mausolea. Guided tours are available (020 8969 0152, www.kensalgreen.co.uk). Many coffins arrived by boat at the ornamental gates set into the railings almost opposite the equally decorative gasometers of Kensal Green Gasworks. There's a huge new Sainsbury's with moorings, cash machines and coffee shop by Bridge 5. Close by is the Canalside Activity Centre (020 8968 4500) bursting with potential activities for kids 10am–5pm Mon–Sat.

Kensal Town *All services (ex banks)*. Ever since St Anne's Dock became Port-a-Bella this has been a popular canal spot. The pub, appropriately called the *Narrowboat*, offers Fullers and bar lunches, barbecues in the summer and frequent chess tournaments! Richard Branson, industrious entrepreneur and balloonist, took Port-a-Bella under his wing with great refurbishment including film studios and mews housing.

Bridge 5–4

Houses back onto the canal, washing flaps on the lines and steamy cooking smells waft out. The *Flora* (Taylor Walker) serves bar meals and has a mooring. The image of Victoriana fades to be replaced by modern thirty-storey highrise flats and the bold curve of the elevated Westway (A40). The *Carlton Bridge Tavern* was rebuilt in 1984/5 and does bar meals.

Please note: Through Central London details in this guide are restricted to matter directly concerning boaters and walkers. For more diverse information we recommend one of the readily available tourist guides. See also the information on Transport For London on page 17 and addresses of London's Tourist Offices on page 15. These and other outlets have excellent guides to public transport available which will help you to make the most of a mooring in this area as a base from which to visit the capital. Perhaps send for information in advance in case you should miss out on any of the theatres, River Thames Cruises, St Paul's Cathedral, The Queen's Gallery at Buckingham Palace . . . etc . . . etc . . . etc!

Those avoiding the better known attractions might try a guided walk from the huge selection, including along the canals, which are on offer every day of the year from Original London Walks (020 7624 3978, www.walks.com).

Harrow Road – Terminus

Edging out from the shadow of Westway the character of the canal undergoes another dramatic transformation. The genteel portico-fronted houses of desirable Maida Vale look out across a canal suddenly blessed with respectability. 'Little Venice'

MAP 32
Paddington Arm – Alperton to Kensal Green

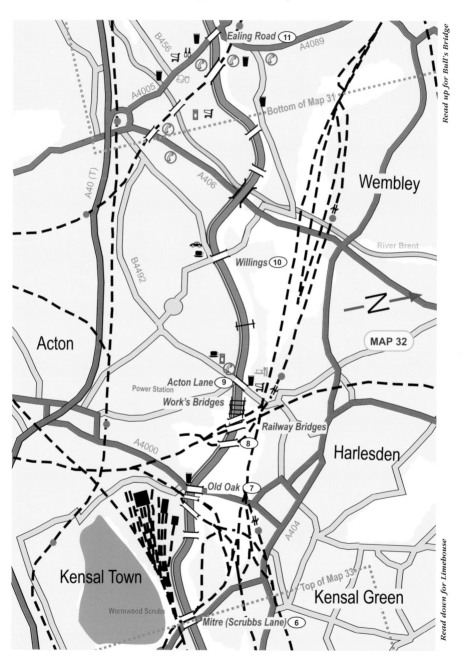

Ealing Road (11)

B456

A4089

A4005

Bottom of Map 31

A40 (T)

A406

Wembley

River Brent

B4492

Willings (10)

MAP 32

Acton

Acton Lane (9)
Power Station

Work's Bridges

Railway Bridges

Harlesden

A4000

8

Old Oak (7)

A404

Kensal Town

Top of Map 33

Kensal Green

Wormwood Scrubs

Mitre (Scrubbs Lane) (6)

Read up for Bull's Bridge

Read down for Limehouse

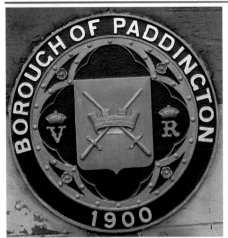

Euan Corrie

Despite the immense changes in this part of London since the canals were a hive of commercial activity, many small pieces of history survive, such as this at Westbourne Terrace.

seems somehow inappropriate and 'Little Amsterdam' would suit better. Houseboats moored along Bloomsbury Road, some bedecked with flowers, are home to several well-known personalities and the passenger boats *Jason's Trip* and the *Lace Plate* are based here too. The former Toll Office at Paddington Stop, now the BW London Region Office, oversees the narrows where working boats were formerly stopped, gauged and toll tickets issued. Squeezing through the 'stop' and under Westbourne Terrace the canal reappears in Browning's Pool, The heart of Little Venice. Beyond the island, to the right, is the Grand Junction's original terminal basin (see page 100).

Little Venice

A somewhat exclusive area of Maida Vale once the busy commercial hub of the Regent's and Paddington canals. When the canal was built packet boats operated from here bringing passengers into the city from the surrounding countryside to the west of London.

British Waterways London Region Office BW has now closed the historic toll office alongside Paddington Stop and no longer has a canalside presence in Central London. The London Region Office is at 1 Sheldon Square, Paddington Central, London W2 6TT (020 7985 7200, Fax 020 7985 7201, e-mail: enquiries.london@britishwaterways.co.uk). This office deals with visitors' moorings along Delamere Terrace and at Camden Lock (registration on arrival, charges for stays of longer than 14 days). Pumpout, by appointment only.

Eating & Drinking Where better to plan an evening out? *Didier* is a first-class French restaurant in Warwick Place where one can still eat reasonably cheaply (open Mon–Fri lunch & eves, Sat eve 020 7286 7484). The *Warwick Castle* next door is a cheerfully respectable London pub serving Bass and Fullers beers, lunches and early evening snacks. Somewhat unusual here is the Canal Café Theatre offering good food, fringe theatre humour and wit in a relaxed and friendly atmosphere. Meanwhile, on the ground floor, is a comfortable Bass Charringtons pub serving bar lunches and evening meals (ex Mon eve). If the boating bug has really bitten, there's the Jason's Restaurant with canalside terrace in warm weather and picture window views of the canal otherwise, and a floating restaurant available for charter between Little Venice and Camden, see below. (Details: 020 7286 6752.)

Jason's Trip Established in 1951 during the Festival of Britain by John James; this is the original canal boat trip. Though Mr James retired in 1972 *Jason's Trip* cruises on, linking Little Venice with Camden Lock, daily Mar–Nov, with a more frequent schedule June–Aug and weekends (020 7286 3428, www.jasons.co.uk). Group and school charter and food available and break of journey at Camden is possible.

The Cascade Art Gallery Housed in the magnificently converted Regent's Canal barge *Crook*, moored in the pool, Alex

MAP 33
Paddington

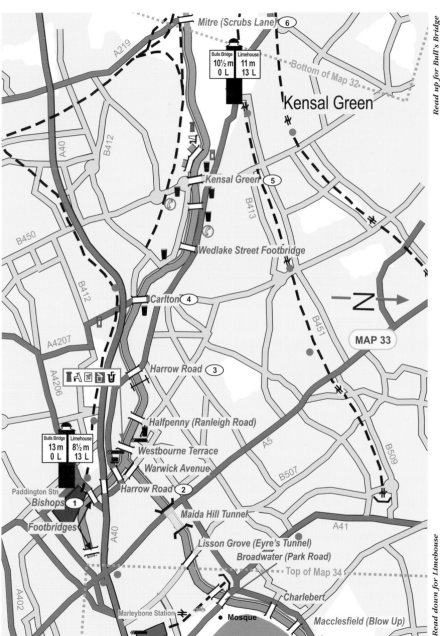

Mitre (Scrubs Lane) ⑥

Read up for Bull's Bridge

Bulls Bridge	Limehouse
10½ m	11 m
0 L	13 L

Bottom of Map 32

Kensal Green

A219

A40

B412

Kensal Green ⑤

B413

B450

Wedlake Street Footbridge

B412

Carlton ④

A4207

N→

A4206

MAP 33

B451

Harrow Road ③

Halfpenny (Ranleigh Road)

Bulls Bridge	Limehouse
13 m	8½ m
0 L	13 L

Westbourne Terrace

A5

Warwick Avenue

B507

Paddington Stn

Bishops ①

Harrow Road ②

B509

Footbridges

Maida Hill Tunnel

A40

A41

Lisson Grove (Eyre's Tunnel)

Broadwater (Park Road)

Top of Map 34

Charlebert

A402

Marleybone Station

Macclesfield (Blow Up)

Mosque

Read down for Limehouse

Euan Corrie

The unusual Regent's Canal lockhouse at Hampstead Road overlooks the teeming activity of modern pubs, clubs and tripboats but the cross paddle gear that connects the two lock chambers remains recognisably the same as painted by Thomas Shepperd in 1823.

Prowse' gallery now combines an exhibition of paintings and prints with the ability to host watercolour courses. Open Thur–Sun, Apr–Oct and at other times by appointment (020 7289 7050, www.alexprowse.com).

A second barge is available for hire for exhibitions and conferences (email: j@littlevenicelondon.co.uk).

Puppet Theatre Barge A converted Thames barge, moored in the pool during the winter and touring during the summer offers a regularly changing programme of puppet shows. Details and bookings: 78 Middleton Road, London, E8 4BP, 020 7249 6876 or 07836 202 755, www.puppetbarge.com.

London Waterbus Company

Operators of the famous Regent's Canal Waterbus, maintaining the service begun in 1959 and running regular public trips between Little Venice, London Zoo and Camden Lock. A special ticket includes zoo entrance. Boats leave hourly, Apr–Oct and winter weekends. Private charter and special public all-day trips to Limehouse and the Lee are available, for which advance booking is essential (Info: 020 7482 2660, Bookings: 020 7482 2550),

The Floating Boater (020 7266 1066, www.floatingboater.co.uk) is also in the Basin. A boat café which is open from lunch until afternoon tea time from which charter trips aboard the converted working boat *Lapwing* may be booked. They also operate the *Prince Regent* for formal cruising lunch or dinner parties, or buffets, up to a maximum of 80 people.

Paddington Basin Before completion of the Regent's Canal in 1820 the Paddington Arm of the Grand Junction ended here and offered the only canal wharfage area in central London. It must have been a very busy place for many years but the once considerable trade has long since disappeared. There have been many redevelopment threats to this now valuable plot of real estate and as this edition of the guide was in preparation work had started. The long-established residential boats have been removed from their moorings at the basin entrance and parts of the water area are being in-filled as towering buildings rise along the north wharf. It remains to be seen whether the water area which survives can form the much-vaunted amenity for canal users or simply be a part of the view from a million office windows. There's another *Grand Junction Arms* on Praed Street. Praed Street is, incidentally, named after William Praed, the first chairman of the Grand Junction Canal Co.

Heading East

Dodging Browning's Island the boater joins the Regent's Canal on the impressively straight approach to Maida Hill Tunnel. An avenue of plane trees and elegant John Nash houses paint a pretty picture, vibrant with colour whatever the season.

Maida Hill Tunnel (272 yards.)

When Mr Portman, the landowner, insisted on a more northerly route under his land he caused more problems than he knew. That it had to be longer than planned was irritating, that it demanded a second 53 yard tunnel under Mr Eyre's land was infuriating, but when engineers encountered shifting sands and a spring, that was expensive. It's rather dank as tunnels go and coming out again is a relief.

Lisson Grove

This is a peculiar area for the canal traveller, who passes through a canyon of high walls, tower blocks and the remains of Marylebone power station. It is possible to moor and climb the spiral staircase to the streets above. Eyre's Tunnel passes beneath Lisson Grove and carries an unusual canal house over its eastern portal. Known locally as the 'upside down' house it has a front door upstairs at street level. A new housing estate has been built on the old goods yard and the commuter-carrying railway passes overhead en-route to Marylebone. The Westminster City Council 'Canalwalk' starts here. In common with canalside walks in Islington and elsewhere, access at bridges is restricted by locking up at dusk. Boaters will discover that their BW service key will fit the locks and are asked to leave the gates as they find them. There's a garage on Park Road.

Lords

The MCC's home and the world's premier cricket ground. Thomas Lord was groundsman to the White Conduit CC and found the new site for the club in 1787. Whites became the MCC in 1811 and moved to Lords in 1814, just as the new Regent's Canal was completed. Open Mon–Fri and match days. The Cricket Memorial Gallery (020 7289 1611) is open match days and by appointment.

Regent's Park

Imagine the rumpus if a motorway went through, say, Woburn Abbey. In 1811 just such a plan was announced; to dig a canal through the heart of Marylebone Park. John Nash was re-laying the Park at the time and was so taken with the idea that he promptly joined the promotional committee. The park commissioners weren't so enthusiastic but respected Nash, so only objected politely, by suggesting that the canal might go round the edge and not through the middle. Agreeing, Nash approached the Prince Regent to ask, that the canal as well as the park might be named after him. Permission was granted, construction began and it was completed in November 1813. Bridges were especially designed to accommodate the park rides and the whole met with genteel approval.

Today we must be grateful for Nash's persistence, since he has rewarded us with the finest length of urban waterway in Britain. Near Broadwater Bridge can be seen the minaret of the Central Islamic Mosque, while opposite are the tidy gardens of elegant, bow-fronted Nuffield Lodge. The canal skirts the park in a delightful leafy cutting, overlooked by the Victorian red and white brick terrace of Prince Albert Road.

Primrose Hill rises to the north and. approaching Cumberland Basin, the canal passes the entrance to London Zoo (open daily from 10am, 020 7722 3333, www.zsl.org.uk). Access is possible only from the road (except by Waterbus – the boat service from Little Venice or Camden Lock runs hourly from 10am in summer, see page 100) but the zoo straddles the canal and boaters can enjoy a free viewing of several displays, including the Snowdon Aviary, opened in 1965.

Regent's Canal – Regent's Park to Camden

Macclesfield or 'Blow-up' Bridge At 5am on the morning of October 2nd 1874, six barges hauled by a steam tug were making their way through the park. The fourth in the train was the *Tilbury*, loaded with nuts, tea, strawboards, some barrels of petroleum and five tons of gunpowder. As she passed under Macclesfield Bridge a huge explosion rent the air, the *Tilbury* disappeared in a fan of splintered timbers and the bridge was totally demolished. The crew were killed instantly, another barge sank, houses were damaged and the explosion woke the population to a radius of 10 or 12 miles. Of Macclesfield Bridge, only the ten iron supporting columns remained. When the bridge was rebuilt, these were re-used and re-erected back to front, so that today rope grooves appear on both sides of the towpath columns – those dating from before the explosion on the side furthest from the water and those from later years on the other.

Places of interest Though it's difficult to moor to a concrete towpath (BW have promised more mooring rings) Regent's Park is a good base for a day out in London. Madame Tussaud's and the Planetarium are on the other side of the park (open daily, 0870 400 3000); the park's Open Air Theatre performs at intervals throughout the summer, and the band plays on Sundays and bank hols. There's a frequent bus service from outside the zoo entrance to Baker Street, etc.

Cumberland Basin A ¾ mile arm departed here to serve Cumberland Hay Market near Euston Road. It was filled in with bomb-site rubble during World War II and now serves as the zoo car park. A length remains for moorings, including the Feng Shang Chinese Restaurant (020 7485 8137).

The canal makes a sharp right-angle bend to leave Regent's Park. A secluded reach with ornate back gardens gives way to reveal industry and the railway from Euston and then incongruous to it all, the Pirate Castle. Passing Gilbey's Gin and a vast warehouse, the canal arrives at Camden, destination of many trip boats from Little Venice.

The Pirate Club A youth organisation founded by the late Lord St Davids in 1966. Originally housed in a converted barge this folly with battlements, arrow slits and drawbridge, was opened in 1977, with a CEGB pumping station opposite built to the same style. The Pirate Club has a boat, the *Pirate Princess* and a fleet of canoes and small craft: beware! The clubhouse is open to visitors 11am–4pm and 4pm–7pm Wed & Thurs. Details (020 7267 6605).

One of the most unusual of London's canal craft must be this Chinese restaurant at Cumberland Basin.

Euan Corrie

MAP 34
Regent's Canal – Regent's Park to City Road

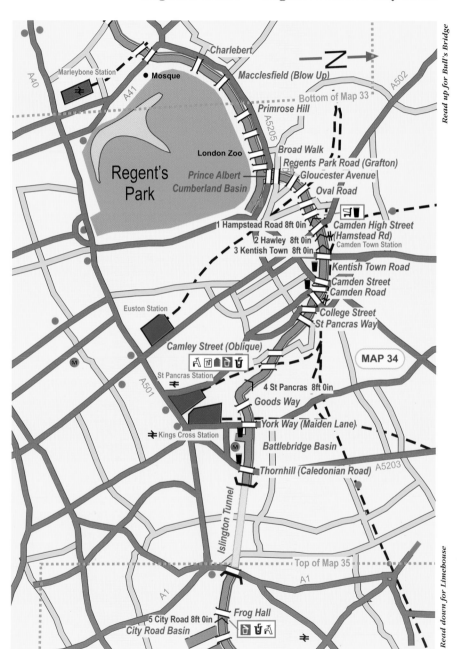

Read up for Bull's Bridge

Charlebert

Marleybone Station

● Mosque

Macclesfield (Blow Up)

Bottom of Map 33

Primrose Hill

London Zoo

Broad Walk

Regents Park Road (Grafton)

Gloucester Avenue

Prince Albert

Oval Road

Regent's Park

Cumberland Basin

1 Hampstead Road 8ft 0in

Camden High Street
(Hamstead Rd)

2 Hawley 8ft 0in

Camden Town Station

3 Kentish Town 8ft 0in

Kentish Town Road

Camden Street

Camden Road

Euston Station

College Street

St Pancras Way

Camley Street (Oblique)

MAP 34

St Pancras Station

4 St Pancras 8ft 0in

Goods Way

Kings Cross Station

York Way (Maiden Lane)

Battlebridge Basin

Thornhill (Caledonian Road)

A5203

Islington Tunnel

Top of Map 35

A1

Read down for Limehouse

5 City Road 8ft 0in

Frog Hall

City Road Basin

Camden *All services.* The town offers all the usual London facilities but it is to Camden Lock that people are drawn. Ever since the old Dingwall's Wharf site was refurbished in 1973 housing a complex of shops, boutiques, market, restaurants and craft workshops the site has bustled with new life. The throng of hangers-on can make working through the locks a hazard but it's a wonderfully vibrant spot always busy with boats and people. If you need supplies head south towards supermarkets and banks. The Round House Theatre (800 yards north) houses London's first Black Arts Theatre. There are pubs and restaurants everywhere.

Eating and Drinking Such a wide choice defeats selection. A pizza house and several take-aways exist nearby. The closest pub is the *Carnarvon Castle* (Taylor-Walker) but there are countless others.

Camden Canal & Narrowboat Association operates the former Grand Union Canal Carrying Co motor boat *Tarporley* to provide day and longer trips for local people, particularly those in any way disadvantaged. Bookings: Sally Bowman, 22 Holmdale Road, London NW6 1BL. (Tel/Fax: 020 7681 7019, www.camden-canals.demon.co.uk).

London Waterbus Company Camden Lock (020 7482 2660). In addition to the standard Waterbus service a special long-distance cruise from Camden to Limehouse and back via Limehouse Cut, River Lee and Hertford Union Canal is run at intervals. Telephone for details.

Camden to St Pancras

Until 1973/74 the locks on the Regent's Canal were paired and pleasure craft needed assistance from lock keepers to make the journey. Converting one lock of each set to an overflow weir made the canal self-regulating and alleviated the need for lock keepers, so pleasure craft can now cruise down unattended. Only Hampstead Road Locks remain as a pair, although with the offside lock out of use. The original pairing

of locks was a compromise intended to save water, based upon the assumption that one would usually be set for the next boat approaching and could serve as a side pond to the other.

Walker's Quay Camden High Street, (020 7485 4433, www.walkersquay.com), immediately below the top lock is not only a restaurant providing snacks or full meals all day but also the base for *Jenny Wren* which offers charter or individually booked public trips and *My Fair Lady* a wide beam cruising restaurant.

Dropping down the locks takes you past the garishly modern MTV studios, commendable for their recognition of a canalside location, and so to Kentish Town Road. The *Devonshire Arms* (Courage, bar meals & pool table) stands on the bridge, together with a variety of shops. Sainsburys is just down the road but the nearby gothic pub will require appropriate dress!

This is an industrial stretch with little greenery and poor access, except unofficially to the A503 and then again onto College Street. The *Prince Albert* public house, takeaway, Post Office and some small shops are sited here, with the *Constitution* beside the towpath at St Pancras Way. It's a Courage pub serving bar food and hosting live music at weekends.

The canal around here was once so busy that entanglements with horse towing lines were common and special steps were provided at particular trouble-spots to enable horses which had been dragged into the canal to be walked out again onto the towing path. Look out for the remains of these inset into the towpath edge.

The canal shrugs off the density of Camden and heads off towards St Pancras, accompanied now by new office-industry and Elm Village, the latter marked by a balcony. There is access at most bridges but it's rarely profitable. Approaching St Pancras the extensive works to redevelop the so called 'King's Cross Railway Lands' have swept away the famous gas holders and many other landmarks.

St Pancras Cruising Club 🍺 ⛵ ⚓ 🏛

🛏 🪣 ♿ St Pancras Basin (020 7278 2805). Slipway (45ft). Visitors and permanent moorings, with electricity supply, by arrangement and welcomes other AWCC members. Bar Wed & Sun lunch, or whenever numbers demand! The oldest canal cruising club in London it was founded in 1962 and continues to organize a busy social and cruising programme.

King's Cross to Islington

This area is subject to huge changes at the time of writing. London's biggest redevelopment scheme since the Blitz of the Second World War is centred on former railway property between and north of King's Cross and St Pancras stations, straddling the canal. This includes provision (many years overdue) of a central London station for services to Europe through the Channel Tunnel. The twin neo-Gothic towers of St Pancras Station, King's Cross' canopy and the Post Office Tower form an impressive backdrop as the canal swings eastwards again. Railway or architecture enthusiasts should not fail to visit W.H. Barlow's trainshed (105ft high, 690ft long and 240ft wide) and the magnificent station buildings at the Midland's St Pancras Terminus or to contrast with the dignified plainness of Cubitt's structures at King's Cross, next door. St Pancras Station is being extensively altered and an additional overall roof extended northwards to accommodate the Eurostar trains which are much longer than any imagined when the station was built. The new structure provides a sharp contrast with its neighbours. There are traces of the several canal arms into the Great Northern Railway's King's Cross Goods yards and warehouses on the offside of the canal. The lines to King's Cross pass under the canal in Gas Works Tunnel here and stop gates were placed either side during the last war to prevent flooding from bomb damage. York Way crosses on Maiden Lane Bridge and there are pubs

Euan Corrie

Winter sunshine highlights the contrast between modern architecture and traditional-style narrowboats at Battlebridge Basin.

and a garage nearby. Immediately after the bridge, which carries some intricate iron work, Battlebridge Basin comes into view on the off side. Battlebridge was the old name for King's Cross and commemorates Boadicea's fight against the Romans. There are more pubs on Caledonian Road, including the *Thornhill Arms* (Charrington) and the *Swan* (Charrington & snacks). The Thornhill Wharf site won a planning award in 1981 as a newly transformed public park and walkers must leave the towpath here to walk over Islington Tunnel (960 yards).

Battlebridge Basin Though some of the warehouses still stand, their purpose changes. John Dickinson, of paper mills fame, had wharves here. Today they are in use as apartments and small industrial units. One of the basin's features is the *Waterside Inn*. Outside, modern red brick; inside a Malvern cider mill complete with oak timbers, coffin boards and woodworm! Bar meals are available. Visitors can moor on the terrace. Booking for traditional Sunday lunch: 0207 7138 613.

London Narrowboat Association
Battlebridge Basin (020 7837 9256). Set up in 1978 as a safe London mooring for narrowboats but accommodates all craft. Visitors welcome and secure overnight moorings by appointment.

London Canal Museum (020 7713 0836, www.canalmuseum.org.uk) is based in an ice warehouse overlooking Battlebridge Basin. It is open 10am–4.30pm Tue–Sun and Bank Holidays. It has displays of the Regent's Canal and ice cream making as well as a good book and souvenir shop.

Islington Tunnel (960 yards). This is London's longest canal tunnel and has no towpath, so walkers will have to take to the roads. Boaters should pass through the tunnel with care – there's a slim possibility of barges coming the other way and there's no room to pass! It passes directly beneath The Angel and Pentonville, a fact not lost on the engineers. Their need to satisfy concerned householders above the tunnel was not helped by unstable subsoil and escalating costs. Extra courses of brick, backfill and tons of cement eventually saw the tunnel completed in 1818, a steam tug working on a continuous chain towed craft through. This was phased out in the 1930s, though a diesel tug still worked the route until a few years ago.

The canal reappears in a deep cutting amid the fashionable refinement of Islington's Georgian quarter. The *Prince of Wales* offers oriental home cooked food at lunchtime and evening on weekdays.

Islington *All services, Tourist Information Centre, 44 Duncan Street (020 7278 8787).* The elegant Georgian terraces are being restored and house values are rising fast. The same can be said of other prices: Camden Passage was a bargain hunter's dream; today it's a nightmare. Mind you, if you're after food and not antiques, then the street market through The Angel is excellent. There are plenty of pubs and restaurants.

City Road By the lock are facilities for boaters and, a little further on, the *Narrowboat*; a generous Charringtons pub with hot lunches, including Sunday roasts, evening snacks (ex Sun) and musicians welcome on Sundays. The two huge basins here, City Road and Wenlock, were both built in the 1820s to supplement facilities at Limehouse. Narrowboats rarely ventured that far (until this century) but collected their cargoes here from dockland lighters. A visitor in 1885 looked down the basin, "with its wharves and carts, its puffing steam barges, its smoking chimneys, the town dimly seen behind it" and approved. Today's visitor sees a mix of dereliction and redevelopment, and hopes. A series of memorable bridges, some brick or iron, others multicoloured, span the canal through to Kingsland but access is not always possible. There are several pubs near Soouthgate Road Bridge: The *Southern Arms* (Courage) has bar food and there's also the *Prince of Wales* and the *Baring Arms*. Slipping between industry and housing, the canal passes Whitmore Road, where there are shops, to arrive at Kingsland. City Road Basin here has been sensibly restored to provide moorings and facilities for boaters.

Islington Narrowboat Association (020 7490 5125, www.inba.org.uk), operates *Angel II*, for day and longer trips by local community groups, schools, senior citizens and private charter with skipper from City Road Basin.

Kingsland *Most services.* There are useful shops, pubs and the Geffrye Museum to prompt a pause here.

The Geffrye Museum (020 7739 9893, www.geffrye-museum.org.uk) dates from 1715, when a group of almshouses was built upon the bequest of Sir Robert Geffrye. It holds an impressive collection

MAP 35
Regent's Canal – Islington

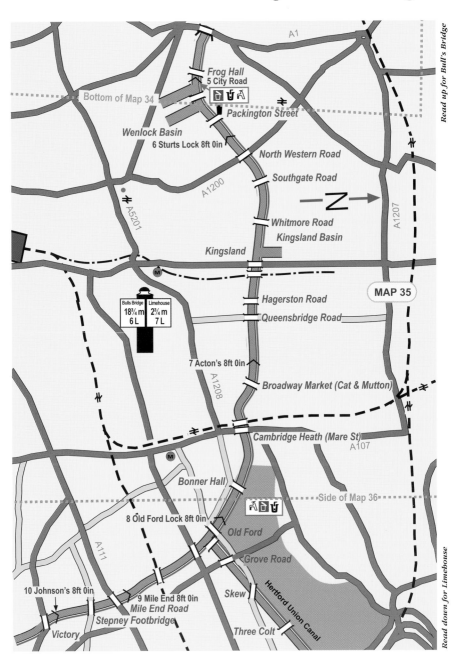

A1

Frog Hall
5 City Road

Bottom of Map 34

Packington Street

Wenlock Basin
6 Sturts Lock 8ft 0in

North Western Road

Southgate Road

A1200

A5201

Whitmore Road
Kingsland Basin

Kingsland

M

A1207

MAP 35

Bulls Bridge | Limehouse
18¾ m | 2¾ m
6 L | 7 L

Hagerston Road

Queensbridge Road

7 Acton's 8ft 0in

A1208

Broadway Market (Cat & Mutton)

Cambridge Heath (Mare St)
A107

M

Bonner Hall

Side of Map 36

8 Old Ford Lock 8ft 0in

Old Ford

A111

Grove Road

10 Johnson's 8ft 0in

9 Mile End 8ft 0in
Mile End Road
Stepney Footbridge

Skew

Hertford Union Canal

Victory

Three Colt

of furniture and domestic equipment, each room reflecting a different period, and offers a fascinating insight into changing patterns and styles. Outside is a walled herb garden. Open Tues–Sun & BH, admission free. Venture further south and you're into Spitalfields (www.spitlfields. org.uk) and area of contrasts, small streets, museums, markets (www.eastlondonmarkets.com), the redeveloped Truman's Brewery, and everything you could wish to eat from bagels to Bangladeshi cuisine.

Kingsland – Acton's Lock

This was formerly an area of decay and decrepit housing but sights of new-found care are evident. Brightest of these are the mosaics and murals, which seem to breed along the canals through London. The colourful mosaics show aspects of canal life as interpreted by Laburnum School.

Laburnum Boat Club (020 7729 2915 www.laburnum.org.uk) between Kingsland and Haggerston bridges, is aimed at youngsters over 9 years of age and offers a wide variety of activities including canoeing and hire of day boats with facilities for the disabled.

Haggerston Offers few obvious facilities for canal users. The *Duke of Sussex* (Whitbread) has a pool table and juke box, but no food.

The steady fall of locks continues, the scenery offering little to excite the imagination. There were huge coalyards here once, as the bricked up dock entrances bear witness.

Bethnal Green *All services.* This area was once famous for the silk weavers of Spitalfields and samples of their work can be seen in the Museum of Childhood, part of the Victoria & Albert (including the roof!). It also contains a large part of that museum's collection of early toys, teddy bears, dolls and dolls-houses. It is open Mon–Thurs, Sat & Sun, admission free (020 8980 2415, www.museu-mofchildhood.co.uk). Access to Cat & Mutton Bridge is from Acton's Lock, access to other facilities at Mare Street.

The sight of Victoria Park is a delightful surprise after what has gone before. This 217 acre park, known as the 'playground of the East End', was laid out in the 1840s by James Pennethorne, a student of Nash, whose opinion of canals was clearly in line with his mentor's. There are moorings, access to the park just above Old Ford Lock and British Waterways have a maintenance yard here.

Globe Town *Shops.* Visit the *Royal Cricketers* (020 8980 3259) canalside pub serving meals. Moorings for patrons on canalside terrace.

Hertford Union Canal

This independent canal was promoted by Sir George Duckett to link the Regent's Canal with the Lee Navigation. Why he bothered is not clear, since within months of its opening in 1830, he was having to offer toll free rates to encourage traffic. By 1848 it was barely navigable and in 1851 Sir George offered it for tender. Nobody wanted it! Eventually the Regent's reconsidered and bought it in 1857, with whom it remained until the formation of the Grand Union network. Its 1¼ miles and three locks (the stop lock is disused) are bordered almost entirely by Victoria Park and offer an unexpectedly attractive route to the Lee (see page 111).

Mile End *(Services on Mile End Road)* The canal's journey through Mile End has improved considerably now that many of the old slums and tenements have been razed and Mile End Park established. At Mile End Lock is access to the main road and the *New Globe*. By Johnson's Lock is the East London Stadium, complete with restaurant and cafe, and another family of gasometers. Passing Salmon Lane Lock, there are a couple of pubs and a Chinese takeaway, the surroundings grow particularly seedy and the view from Commercial

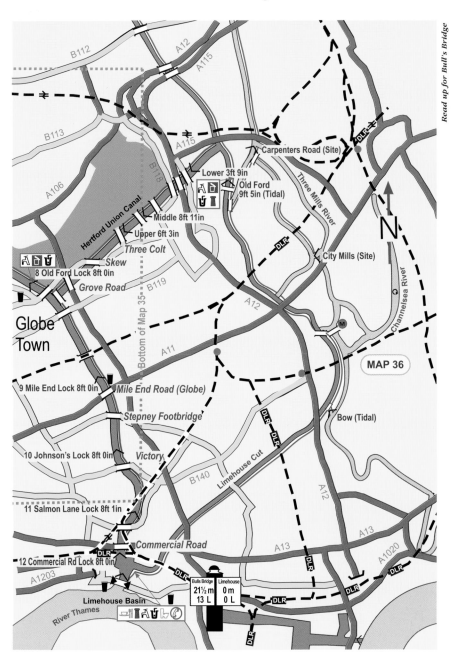

MAP 36

Regent's Canal – Limehouse

Read up for Bull's Bridge

B112

A12

A115

B113

A115

Carpenters Road (Site)

Lower 3ft 9in

Old Ford
9ft 5in (Tidal)

Hertford Union Canal

B118

Middle 8ft 11in

Upper 6ft 3in

Three Colt

DLR

City Mills (Site)

Skew

8 Old Ford Lock 8ft 0in

Grove Road

B119

Three Mills River

Channelsea River

N

M

MAP 36

**Globe
Town**

Bottom of Map 35

A11

A12

9 Mile End Lock 8ft 0in   *Mile End Road (Globe)*

Stepney Footbridge

DLR
DLR

Bow (Tidal)

10 Johnson's Lock 8ft 0in   *Victory*

B140

Limehouse Cut

A12

11 Salmon Lane Lock 8ft 1in

Commercial Road

DLR

12 Commercial Rd Lock 8ft 0in

A1203

A13

A13

A1020

DLR

DLR

DLR

Limehouse Basin

Bulls Bridge	Limehouse
21½ m	0 m
13 L	0 L

DLR

River Thames

Limehouse

Euan Corrie

Modern housing stands on top of the Limehouse Link road tunnel on what was part of the Regent's Canal Dock. A wide variety of inland and sea-going craft occupy pontoon moorings in the basin as a Docklands Light Railway Train crosses the viaduct above Commercial Road Lock.

Road Lock is all the more awesome because of it (though anything less commercial you'll rarely see).

Limehouse Basin formerly Regent's Canal Dock, was a busy transhipment dock between steamers, barges and narrowboats. It has been redeveloped to provide offices and luxury apartments. This included infilling of part of the basin and construction of the Limehouse Link tunnel which passes beneath. Pleasure boat moorings are available, but it is unlikely that the Dock will ever again see commercial use, especially since the ship entrance lock from the Thames has been reduced in size.

The Cruising Association 🛏 🔥 🚻 📶
🔌 📞 🚾 ☎ 1 Northey St, Limehouse Basin, London E14 8BT (0207 537 2828, www.cruising.org.uk, VHF Channel 80), operates the long term and temporary moorings in the basin. There are also showers here. Boat Safety Scheme inspections can be arranged and breakdowns dealt with. The Association has a bar and restaurant open during traditional pub hours and organises lectures and meetings to which non-members are welcome. The office is open 9.30am–5.30pm Mon–Fri and 9am–5pm at weekends.

Limehouse Lock The lock giving access to the Thames is tidal but is manned between 8am and 5pm daily. The lock measures 30m x 8m x 3m on sill. Boats wishing to join or leave the Thames are recommended to notify the Dock Master in advance by telephoning 020 7308 9930. Contact can also be made of VHF Channel 74. A swing bridge carries Narrow Street across the lock tail and will require opening at certain tide levels and for larger vessels. Boaters are asked to obey the bridgekeeper's instructions.

Vessels entering Limehouse Basin from the Thames require a British Waterways licence, the issue of which will require proof of the possession of a Boat Safety Certficate and third party insurance. Those seeking temporary haven in the dock, but not intending to navigate further should contact the Dock Master. It should be noted that rubbish carried into the dock and Limehouse Lock by the tide can be hazardous to small craft. Boaters arriving off Limehouse outside lock opening times will find moorings very limited and uncomfortable.

When planning a circular cruise around London's waterways it is best to navigate down the Regent's Canal and up the Thames to join the Grand Union Canal at Brentford rather than the other way around. (A comprehensive timetable for the availability of these and London's other tidal locks is available from any BW office in London, see page 15, or from the lock keepers at Teddington Lock.)

Sustenance There are several excellent pubs to find: By Limehouse Lock is the *Barley Mow*, a Taylor-Walker pub housed in the restored Dockmaster's House. Meals are available all day. Children are welcome and there's a riverside terrace. The *Grapes* (east along Narrow Street) is listed in Routiers guide for its speciality of seafood dishes (Mon–Fri lunch, Mon–Sat eve and Sunday lunch), whilst further along is *The House They Left Behind*, a quaint little Watney's pub serving home-cooked food Mon–Sat and Sun lunch, with live entertainment Sun eve. Opposite, *Booty's Riverside Bar* (originally the *Waterman's Arms*) offers food Mon–Fri and splendid views over Limehouse Reach.

Limehouse Cut

This 1½-mile canal predates the Regent's by more than 40 years, having been planned in 1767 and completed in 1770. It was a vital link for the river Lee, itself navigable since before the 15th century, as it provided a valuable short cut between the Pool of London and Bow Creek, bypassing the Isle of Dogs. Originally it entered the river just downstream of Limehouse Basin but, in 1968, a new link was dug that joined directly with the basin. The cut is part tidal and skippers of craft deeper than narrow canal

boats may find it advisable to check with British Waterways concerning the state of tides, levels and traffic (020 7308 9930). During extreme tides a barrier will be lowered into the cut and passage prohibited, so do check.

The Lee is legally a commercial waterway but barge traffic is almost non-existent. Bow Locks themselves are operable from 4hrs before to 2hrs after high water (booking is necessary 020 7987 5661) but this route to/from the Thames is not suitable for light craft or for the inexperienced. (A comprehensive timetable for the availability of these and London's other tidal locks is available from any BW office in the London area, see page 15, or from the lock keepers at Teddington Lock.)

Euan Corrie

Even the much reduced lock chamber, which was built inside the original Regent's Canal Dock Ship Lock chamber, can appear to be a daunting size from the deck of a canal boat waiting to leave the Thames tideway. It has radial gates which allow rapid filling and emptying without the complications of any paddle gear.

River Lee Navigation

The river Lee is navigable from the Thames tideway at Bow Creek, through Bow Locks to Fielde's Weir, where the river Stort joins, as far as Hertford. The navigable Stort extends to Bishop's Stortford. Some research, consideration of tides and local advice is necessary before attempting to explore the numerous backwaters and interconnecting rivers around Bow and Stratford but the main river between the junctions of the Hertford Union Canal and Limehouse Cut makes an interesting diversion from the Regent's Canal. The high spot of this short urban voyage is perhaps Three Mills at Bromley-by-Bow, the UK's largest tide mill. The House Mill is open on Sundays May –Oct and Saturdays Jun–Sept (01992 702200, www.leevalleypark.com.)

Thames Tideway

The navigation authority for the tidal river Thames through London is the Port of London Authority (PLA). The PLA publishes a booklet titled *Pleasure Users Guide to the Tidal Thames* and a map *The Tidal Thames for Leisure and Pleasure*, copies of which should be obtained in advance of a tidal passage by canal craft (see Useful Addresses, page 15).

Suitably powered and equipped boats can navigate the Thames tideway between Limehouse Basin and the Grand Union Canal at Brentford or the Thames (non-tidal) Navigation at Teddington. Boaters should take advantage of the flood tide to reach the river's higher reaches but must beware of fast tidal flows and large baulks of driftwood in the tideway. Although commercial shipping and river lighterage has drastically declined on the Thames in London, large vessels, including visiting warships, and trains of barges under tow may still be encountered navigating the river above Tower Bridge. Boaters should keep well clear of such large craft under way or moored at buoys in the river. The tidal Thames can thus be dangerous for small craft so canal boaters should proceed onto the river with caution, be suitably equipped and keep a good look-out.

About the only non-tidal mooring between Limehouse Basin and Brentford where pleasure craft are welcome is St Katharine Haven just downstream from Tower Bridge on the north bank of the river (the former St Katharine Dock). Access through the lock here is 2 hours before and 1½ hours after high water at London Bridge.

St Katharine Haven 🛇 ⚓ 🅿 (020 7481 8350, www.stkaths.co.uk). 50 St Katharine's Way, London E1W 1LA.

The General Directions for Navigation in the Port of London 1991 came into force on 1st June and include the requirement for VHF radios on all boats over 20 metres (66ft) using the tidal Thames below Teddington. The Thames Navigation Service point out that this was always an 'understood' rule but not enforced until the current General Directions came into force. The radios must be capable of communicating with the Thames Navigation Service. Copies of the General Directions can be obtained free from the Thames Navigation Service, Royal Pier, Gravesend, Kent DA12 2BG (01474 322010).

Those wishing to see the Thames without taking navigational responsibility are strongly recommended to the many trip boats which offer a wide variety of timings and routes – details are easily obtained from the *Mayor of London's Thames River Boat Service Guide* which may be obtained from Tourist Offices or Transport For London (see page 17).